Date: 3/22/11

the dark side
of innocence

Also by Terri Cheney

Manic: A Memoir

terri cheney

the dark side of innocence

growing up bipolar

ATRIA BOOKS

New York   London   Toronto   Sydney

ATRIA BOOKS
A Division of Simon & Schuster, Inc.
1230 Avenue of the Americas
New York, NY 10020

To the best of my ability, I have re-created events, locales, people, and organizations from my memories of them. In order to maintain the anonymity of others, in some instances I have changed the names of individuals and places, and the details of events. I have also changed some identifying characteristics, such as physical descriptions, occupations, and places of residence.

First Atria Books hardcover edition March 2011

ATRIA BOOKS and colophon are trademarks of Simon & Schuster, Inc.

For information about special discounts for bulk purchases, please contact Simon & Schuster Special Sales at 1-866-506-1949 or business@simonandschuster.com.

The Simon & Schuster Speakers Bureau can bring authors to your live event. For more information or to book an event, contact the Simon & Schuster Speakers Bureau at 1-866-248-3049 or visit our website at www.simonspeakers.com.

Manufactured in the United States of America

10   9   8   7   6   5   4   3   2   1

Library of Congress Cataloging-in-Publication Data is available.

ISBN 978-1-4391-7621-4
ISBN 978-1-4391-7625-2 (ebook)

To my mother

the dark side of innocence

Introduction

There's a beast out there, and it's preying on children. I didn't know this when I was growing up. I only knew that there was something very, very wrong with me. It wasn't until 1994, when I was thirty-four years old, that I finally found the right name for it: bipolar disorder.

After years of secretly struggling with the disease, I wrote a book about my experience. *Manic: A Memoir* was published in 2008. It describes my life as a Beverly Hills entertainment attorney—outwardly successful, representing the likes of Michael Jackson, Quincy Jones, and major motion picture studios. But behind the carefully poised façade was a string of bloody suicide attempts, nights in jail, repeated hospitalizations, and ruined relationships. When I was depressed, I was completely paralyzed, literally hiding out under my desk. But when I was manic, I made up for the lost time with dazzling productivity, charisma, and boundless energy.

I told no one about my illness back then—not my friends, my family, my coworkers; no one except my doctors. With the publication of *Manic*, of course, the whole world was going to be privy to my secret. I rationalized this by telling myself that no one was really going to care. Who could possibly be interested in my messy, chaotic blur of a life?

I was wrong.

To my everlasting surprise, *Manic* hit the *New York Times* best-seller list a month after its release. As of this writing, it is in its tenth printing, has been translated into eight foreign languages, and was even optioned by HBO for a television series, the ultimate stamp of pop culture approval. Don't misunderstand me: I love my book, I think it's a very good book, and I worked seven long years on it. But I also know that its success has little to do with my writing. The time has finally come for awareness: the world seems to have a rampant curiosity about bipolar disorder. Almost without exception, everyone I've talked to either knows or knows of someone with this disease (or has it themselves).

I was completely unprepared for the torrent of emails I received: the outpouring of gratitude, the baring of souls. But what moved me the most, what I kept coming back to over and over again, were the emails from parents of bipolar children. They were heartrending, passionate, and unapologetically hungry for information. Why were their children acting like this? Did I understand the symptoms? Did I know of a cure? The love was palpable, as was the desperation.

In many of these emails, and in the numerous interviews, readings, and lectures I've given since, the same question kept popping up, without fail: How old was I when I realized that something was seriously wrong with me? I remember the first time I answered this question. It was during a live radio show, and I was nervous. My mind flashed immediately to a prolonged bout of depression I suffered when I was sixteen years old. "Sixteen," I quickly replied. New authors get a little glib with repetition, and "sixteen" soon became my stock answer. But deep down, I knew that wasn't right. My early childhood wasn't just a strange one; it was a sick one, and there was more to the story than I was willing to tell.

Then in May of '08, shortly after my book came out, I visited New York City for a reading. I was in a downtown subway station when I spotted a bright red *Newsweek* banner and, in bold type, the cover story: "Growing Up Bipolar." I devoured that article. I was shocked to learn that at least eight hundred thousand children in the United States have been diagnosed as bipolar. (I've since seen estimates of over a million.) I would later learn from a *New York Times Magazine* cover article that there has been a fortyfold increase in the diagnosis in recent years—a whopping 4,000 percent increase since the mid-1990s, according to National Public Radio.

The very next day, I was sitting in my editor's office, discussing what to write next. My editor looks like a

Pre-Raphaelite angel, which is disconcerting enough. But then out of the blue, just like that, she said, "What about your childhood?"

I froze. "What about it?"

"Lots of people seem curious. You don't mention it much in *Manic*, you know."

There's a very good reason for that: I wanted people to buy the book. Difficult as it was for me to imagine anyone caring about the exploits of my bipolar adulthood, I found it even harder to conceive of anyone being interested in my morass of a childhood. At least when I was an adult, I had a name for what was wrong with me: manic depression. It's easier to make sense of things—even very disturbing things like sexual acting out and suicidality—when there's a big, fat label slapped on top. But as a child, I knew nothing. I had no diagnosis. All I had was a vague and gnawing awareness that I was different from other children, and that different was not good. Different must be kept hidden.

"I don't think I can remember back that far," I said, glancing away from Sarah's eyes to the concrete block of a building across the way.

It was part evasion, part truth. Memory has always been a tricky business with me, especially since the twelve rounds of electroshock therapy I went through in 1994. I write what I remember as honestly and accurately as I can. But I'm never quite sure that what I remember is what other people see as "true." Mental illness has its own lens.

"That's exactly what you said about *Manic*, and yet you

managed." Sarah paused, and the silence drew me back in to her. "I think you should try."

I left her office that afternoon convinced that I would send a polite but discouraging email in a couple of days. But she got me thinking, which is what a good editor is supposed to do. And thinking. And eventually, jotting down glimpses of the past. I pored over what mementos I still have of my childhood: some photos, early writings, a cherished keepsake or two. I plagued my mother and brother with questions (my father, unfortunately, died in 1997): Did this really happen? Did I really do that? Fragments gradually became paragraphs, images evolved into scenes. Once I started to remember, windows that I thought were welded shut flew open. I may not have recalled the exact dialogue spoken at the dinner table, but I couldn't forget the feelings. I was seven years old all over again, and frankly, it was terrifying.

Childhood bipolar disorder is a lot like adult bipolar disorder in that it's a never-ending battle of cycling moods: up, down, in between, and all across the emotional spectrum. Mania brings euphoria, agitation, grandiosity, recklessness. You feel invulnerable, ecstatic, as if you could move the world without a lever. And yet, surprisingly, mania is not that much fun. Your senses are too acute; other people think and move too slowly for your pleasure. You blithely bulldoze over them in search of the next sensation.

Depression is more familiar to most people. It's not just the blues, it's so much worse: a bleakness beyond reason. There is no light, there is no hope, there is only this moment of inarticulate despair that you know at your core will last forever. When I'm depressed, I simply can't move. It's an effort to blink, to breathe, even to cry. The only thing that really soothes me, strangely enough, is suicidal ideation.

There are other mood states in between mania and depression: hypomania, for example, which is that glorious period that sometimes precedes mania. You're charming, creative, and energetic, without mania's impaired judgment. You seem to cast a magic spell wherever you go: other people are drawn to you, and you're absolutely fascinated by everything and anything they have to say. It's the best part of being bipolar.

But there's also the bizarre "mixed state," where the worst of depression and mania collide. You feel utterly despondent but possessed by a tremendous, surging energy. I know I'm in a mixed state when all I want to do is shatter glass. Not surprisingly, it's the state in which the most suicides occur.

If this sounds overwhelming, it is. But so much more is known about adult bipolar disorder than about its incarnation in childhood. From what I've discovered in my research, there are significant differences. In adulthood, over the course of years, and with the luxury of perspective, patterns eventually emerge. In my case, for example, I've learned that now I will usually experience three days of mania followed by four days of depression, and varying periods of relative normalcy in between. This is what's known as "rapid cycling," and it's unusual because the majority of people spend weeks or months in a particular mood state before switching to another.

In children, however, moods often fluctuate like hummingbirds' wings. One minute they're up, the next they're down, and there seems to be no clear delineation between the two phases. Rapid cycling is far more common in children than in adults, and of course, it's much more difficult to treat: like chasing a comet's tail. Mixed states are also more common in children, which wrings my heart because they are so agonizing.

And there seems to be a qualitative difference in the experience of mania: agitation, irritability, and anger are more pronounced in childhood mania than the classic adult euphoria. But many manic traits, unfortunately, remain the same. For example, many parents report that their bipolar children are strangely hypersexual. They exhibit an awareness of and preoccupation with sex that belies their essential innocence. This was certainly true in my case.

I can hear the skeptical reader now: children are naturally moody. Teenagers are even worse. Given the inherent volatility of childhood and the volcanic eruptions of adolescence, how can you tell when it's bipolar disorder? It's a very good question. Early-onset bipolar disorder is notoriously difficult to diagnose, even by the most seasoned professionals. It mimics many other conditions, like attention deficit/hyperactivity disorder (ADHD), oppositional defiant disorder, or plain old unipolar depression.

While it's extremely hard to discern a pattern of cycling moods in what looks and feels like chaos, it's clear that parents and doctors must at least be cognizant of the possibility of bipolar disorder—if only to rule it out. Treatment for other conditions (stimulants and antidepressants, for example) may seriously exacerbate bipolar symptoms.

I don't intend this book to be a primer on early-onset bipolar disorder, nor do I profess to be an expert on the disease. I can't tell you if your child is bipolar. I can only offer my own experience. Looking back at my childhood and comparing it with the madness I wrote about in *Manic*, it seems clear to me that the seeds of insanity were already planted at a very early age. But how much of this book is about growing up bipolar, and how much is just about growing up? I can't answer this question. I don't think anyone can.

So I'm putting my story down for all the parents who have asked me, so plaintively, "What was your own childhood like?" Maybe there will be clues in here; maybe even some answers. I suspect that at most there may be recognition, and I hope that will translate to this knowledge: if you are the parent of a bipolar child or if you are bipolar yourself, you are not alone.

Terri Cheney
Los Angeles, California

1

A little boy died
When he was seven.
He went straight up
To Heaven.
                    —My version of a nursery rhyme, age seven

Killing yourself at any age is a seriously tricky
business. But when I was seven, the odds felt insurmountable.
My resources were so limited, after all. We lived in a one-story
house, so there was nowhere to jump. The cabinet where the
good silver was kept—the one with the knives that could make a
nice, clean slice—was locked, and my mother had the key. We

did have a swimming pool in our backyard, but who was going to teach me how to drown? I'd only just learned how to dog paddle.

It all started two nights before my seventh birthday, after a fight with my brother, Zach. I was a delicate-looking thing, pale as porcelain, with long red hair that flowed down to the middle of my back. Zach was ten, and big for his age. I didn't care.

"You're sitting in my chair," I said.

Zach didn't stop eating. "So?" he mumbled.

"Move."

"You move."

I could hear my voice growing shrill. "Move."

"No, you move."

My mother intervened. "Honey, let Zach sit next to his dad for a change. You come sit next to me." She patted the empty chair to her right.

Except for fancy occasions like Thanksgiving, we always had our meals at the L-shaped kitchen counter. My father would sit at the head; I'd sit next to him; then my mother; then Zach. I don't know who had assigned these places, but that was how it had always been.

I felt my hand tighten into a fist. I could just go back to my room. I wasn't that hungry anyway. But something deep inside me kept me standing there, transfixed. That something was so familiar, so real and omnipotent, I'd given it a name: the Black Beast.

I tried to negotiate.

"Not now," I argued.

"Now," the Black Beast insisted.

My fingers clenched tighter, so hard that my nails gouged into my palms.

Daddy hadn't come home from work yet, so his chair was empty. There was still time to fix this, if indeed it needed fixing. You could never tell with Zach. Of everyone in my family, I felt that he was the only one really keeping track of things. At ten, he could already see straight through me. He knew I was not adorable.

I gave him fair warning. "Zach, I swear, if you don't move now, you're gonna be sorry."

He ignored me and reached for a tortilla chip, his hand passing right in front of me. Big mistake.

I grabbed the nearest fork and stabbed, hard, into his flesh. There was a moment's bloody satisfaction, like when you bite into a good, rare piece of steak and the juices flood through your mouth. The fork stood up straight from the back of Zach's hand. I'd skewered him like a bullfighter.

My mother swore and ran to get the first aid kit while Zach screamed. Thank God she was a registered nurse and knew exactly what to do. I don't remember much of what followed—just that I was sent to my room, where I waited in terror for my father to come home.

It was the night of December 5, 1966. It was a good time to live in suburban Southern California. Building was booming, but you could still drive a mile or two out of town and picnic in orange groves. The smog was bad, but it produced brilliant sunsets. Out in the real world—the grown-up world I only caught whiffs of now and then—trouble was brewing: in four years, words like "Kent State" and "Cambodia" would enter the national consciousness. The Beatles would break up, Janis Joplin and Jimi Hendrix would die.

But in Ontario, the little corner of the world where I lived, some forty-odd miles east of LA, none of that seemed to matter. Euclid Avenue, the eucalyptus-lined main street of town, was named one of the seven most beautiful avenues in the United States, and a good Sunday still consisted of church and a stroll beneath the trees. No one knew then that a blight was about to kill them all off, one after the other. In 1966, all was green and thriving.

Things weren't exactly perfect at 1555 North Elm Court, but you couldn't tell from the outside. The garage was freshly painted, the pink geraniums my mother had planted on a whim were blooming, and a brand-new fire-engine red Dodge Comet stood in the driveway, waiting for us to hop in. But come around midnight, and you might hear a different story: voices brittle as icicles, aiming for the heart. I could hear them through my bedroom door, although I couldn't quite make out the words. Something about money, usually; and sometimes, when the frost was particularly thick, the single word *Rebecca*. On those nights, I fully expected to wake up and find all the pink geraniums withered and dead. But to my surprise, they continued to bloom, and the neighbors looked on us as a fine family.

And so we were. Zach was tall for his age and strapping, with a shock of red hair even more vibrant than my own. My mother and father were both handsome people, trim and photogenic. In the few pictures I possess of us, we look like a Kodak commercial: smiling, smiling, smiling. I remember hating being photographed as a child, and perhaps that accounts for my awkward grin. But even I could look angelic when I chose.

"There's something wrong with her."

My mother's normally cool, firm voice quavered. She was either on the edge of tears or extremely angry, I couldn't tell which. I pressed my ear up against the crack in the den door, trying to listen harder.

"There's nothing wrong with her. She's only seven. Besides, she's number one in her class." My father's Kansas twang was followed by a crackle; no doubt a page of the *Daily Report* being turned.

"Put that goddamned paper down and listen to me. You call what she did to Zach tonight normal?"

Another crackle, then silence. "She won't do anything like that again. I'll make her give me her word."

My mother laughed. It was not a pleasant sound. "She'd say anything to get you to forgive her. I mean it, Jack, I'm worried. One minute she's sweet as pie, the next she's a little fiend. And all those days she claims she's sick when she really isn't—"

"That's just to stay out of school. All kids do that."

"Not for weeks at a time. I tell you, something's wrong with her."

I heard the sound of a cup or a fist banging down on the table. "Nothing's wrong with my baby. Christ, she's number one in her class."

"You already said that."

"Well, it's true, isn't it?"

There was a moment's silence, and then my mother began to cry. She rarely cried, except when she was so frustrated she couldn't find the words to express herself.

"You always take her side," she said.

"There are no sides here," my father said, his voice softening. "It's just us."

"I don't know how to handle her anymore. And it's not fair to Zach." My mother was openly sobbing now.

"Shhh," my father said. "If there's a problem, I'll fix it. You know I always do."

I was glad I was only eavesdropping. I couldn't have stood the sight of my mother's tears. I crept back to bed, deeply ashamed of whatever was so clearly "wrong" with me.

Wrong with me, wrong with me. I knew my mother was right, of course; I'd always known I was different from other kids. I just didn't realize how much it showed. How was my father going to "fix it"? What would they do to me if they ever found out how bizarre I really was? It wouldn't just be a matter of being grounded then. They'd take me away and lock me up somewhere, and I'd never see my daddy again. I'd have to be more careful.

"Careful," I whispered into my pillow.

My father stood in my bedroom doorway. There was a crease on his forehead that I'd never seen before.

"Why did you do it?" he asked.

"He made me do it," I said with as much bravado as I could muster. How could I begin to explain what I didn't understand myself? My father couldn't possibly know, because I couldn't possibly tell him, that "he" did not refer to Zach. "He" was the Black Beast, the monster that ruled over me and manipulated my moods. The Black Beast didn't live under my bed or in the closet, like a proper childhood monster should. He lived inside my heart and head, leaving little room for hope or joy or any emotion lighter than sorrow. Sometimes he weighed a zillion trillion tons, and it was all I could do just to breathe.

But then at other times, the Black Beast switched my mood in exactly the opposite direction. I'd be agitated, irritable, giddy, and silly, all in quick succession. One minute the prick of a tag on the back of my sweater would make me writhe and scream; the next I'd be roaring with laughter at my own private jokes and pirouetting down the aisles of the supermarket. Those were "Disneyland days," as my father called them, and although life in an amusement park can be exhausting, I still preferred them to the days in the dark.

Most children have a secret friend. But I never considered the Black Beast my friend. He was bigger than any mere child-hood whim: he was a living, breathing creature that inhabited my body. I couldn't just stuff him away in the toy chest and sit on the lid.

We fought constantly. I didn't always want to do or say or feel the things that he commanded, because they often got me into trouble. But he was stronger than I was, and very persuasive. I'd originally named him "Black Beauty," after one of my favorite bedtime stories, in an attempt to make him seem more like a pet. It didn't work. When the Black Beast wanted his way with me, there was simply no stopping him.

I didn't dare tell my father about this—or anyone else, for that matter. I thought that no one could possibly want a child possessed by a beast. So I cried that night instead: big, gulping sobs, bigger than my mother's, because I needed my father's allegiance more than she did. She was so attractive, she could get any man she wanted. I was a scrawny almost-seven-year-old, and there was nowhere else to turn. I shook off the covers and held out my arms. "I'm so sorry, Daddy," I said.

He came over and sat on the edge of my bed. "Do you promise never to do anything like that again?"

I nodded, crying harder. Daddy looked around and picked up Toto from the foot of my bed. Toto was the tattered stuffed dog I'd had since I was three, my constant ally, my dearest friend.

"Swear on Toto," he said.

"I swear," I said. The sobs were coming so thick and fast by then that I could barely get the words out. And then at last—at last—my father took me in his arms and pressed me to his chest. My breathing slowed down instantly, the throbbing in my neck and temples eased. But just as my tears began to subside and I felt the universe slip back into its proper orbit, he held me out at arm's length and shook his head. "You know, I'm very disappointed in you," he said. "I want you to lie here and think about that for a while." Then he got up and went back to the den.

I clutched Toto and thought about it. Thought about it, hard. There were really only two avenues open to me:

1. I could win back my father's love, or
2. I could die.

Don't ask me how I knew about suicide at such a tender age. The Black Beast knew all sorts of things that were better left unknown. I was fascinated by death; always had been. The nuns thought it was wonderful that I studied my catechism so intently, but the truth was, to me the Bible was just a great grisly story. The same was true of fairy tales: I wolfed them down. Not the saccharine Disney versions, but the unexpurgated Grimms, with their sawed-off heels and lopped-off heads and altogether dark and nasty vision. It satisfied something deep and hungry inside me to know that there was a way out of this life.

At the moment, though, it seemed easier just to try to win back Daddy's love. I'd done it before — I knew how. Winning back my father's love meant getting an A-plus at something. Not an A, mind you. Mere As were for ordinary folk who didn't have that extra special something it took to rise above the pack. My father made it clear to me: every A-plus earned crisp dollar bills, while straight As merited only pocket change.

I applied desperate logic. It seemed to me that all my father really lived for was my outstanding progress in school. He never talked much about his work as a real estate developer; he had no hobbies that I knew of; and when he came home, my mother greeted him with warmed-over argument. But he'd sit for hours in his brown leather chair, listening to me talk about my latest achievement, his face intent and a proud-to-bursting smile lighting his eyes. Nothing my mother said could disturb him then. "Jack, the gas bill's overdue." "Jack, your meat loaf's getting cold." "Jack, did you hear me? I'm talking to you."

So I figured I must be the reason he kept coming home. Narcissistic? Perhaps. But there must have been some truth to it. No doubt he loved my mother and Zach, but he seemed to love those A-pluses best of all. I don't know what they meant to him; I only knew the light in his eyes.

But how to get the A-plus? I looked over at the blank sheet of construction paper lying on my desk—my latest homework assignment—and shuddered. How could I possibly ace it? Everything was wrong, all wrong. The paper wasn't supposed to be white, it was supposed to be manila and marked across with thin blue lines so that I could print neatly between them. That was how it had always been; that was how it was supposed to be.

I'd told my parents about my dilemma, calmly as I could, and they'd searched the local stationery stores for lined manila paper, with no luck. Finally, my mother wound up buying the offending blank white paper, and for a moment I considered blaming her for my predicament. But deep down I knew it wasn't her fault—it was mine. I was the one who had claimed to be too sick to go to school for the seventh day running, so I wasn't there to pick up the special paper that went along with the assignment.

All my mother knew was what she had heard over the phone from Sister Mary Bernadette: write a story about yourself and draw a picture to illustrate it. But how could I tell a proper story without the little blue lines? My handwriting wasn't anywhere near good enough yet; it would sprawl all over the page. The result would be . . . catastrophe. I'd get a C—maybe even a C-minus.

No. Never. Death first.

It never occurred to me that my thoughts might be a little extreme. I knew what I knew: I had to stay the head of my class. That was what held the fabric of my existence together: I had to be the best. The smartest, the most promising, the one to keep an eye on, the one to come home for. So there was really no other option left. If an A-plus was impossible, I'd simply have to die.

A shiver of fear ran through my body. I knew what death looked like, from having come across my pet mouse Jitsy last year, lying stiff and motionless in her cage. Her little red eyes were closed. I poked her and tried to shake her awake. When she didn't respond, I ran to find my father.

"It's not that kind of sleep," he explained, gingerly picking her up by her tail and laying her in a shoe box. "Jitsy won't be waking up."

I was only five then, and I didn't understand. "How come?"

"She's gone to Heaven," my father said.

Heaven I understood. We'd learned all about it in school. Heaven was the place where good souls went to eat as much ice cream as they wanted the whole day long. Of course, there was that other place, but I didn't want to think about it. Zach had shown me pictures from his third grade catechism: bodies twisted and tormented, writhing in pain while the flesh on their bones roasted as crisp as Kentucky Fried Chicken.

I jumped into bed and jerked the covers up over my head. In spite of my mother's frequent warnings about wasting electricity, I didn't turn off my lamp. Some things, like bad grades and Hell, were best left to the light.

I slept fitfully the rest of that evening, with snatches of dreams that would have made the Grimm Brothers proud. Then all at once my eyes fluttered open, and I was wide awake. I glanced over at my bookshelf, at my rapidly growing collection of the lives of saints. Not that I expected to be named a saint after my death. That dream would have to die along with me, because I knew full well that killing yourself was a sin. It was, after all, a terrible theft: the theft of God's power over when to end a life. But I was clever. I had a plan.

It was all in the timing.

The way I understood it, before the age of seven, a child is considered free of sin. The soul is virgin territory then, innocent and unblemished. And here's the kicker: so long as the child dies before she turns seven, she goes straight to Heaven. No messing around with purgatory, no chance of the devil getting a taste. Straight. To. Heaven.

I figured that qualified as an A-plus at death, and I was going to get it. Which posed a problem: I had only one day left to do the deed. I twisted around to look at the clock: just after five in the morning. Normally, I liked to take my time with things—figure out all the angles, meticulously check for errors—but I didn't have that luxury. This would have to be a smash-and-grab operation. I knew where my mother kept her pills, the little blue ones she took every morning. They were in the very top drawer of her bureau, where she kept all her "unmentionables." I wasn't allowed to go in her bureau. I wasn't even allowed to go in her bedroom, which she kept locked. But every once in a while, when she was in a particularly good mood, she'd let me in to watch her dress.

Watching my mother get dressed to go out for the evening was a bewitching experience. She'd start with a spritz of Arpège behind her knees and build from there, sliding into a pair of transparent silk stockings and snapping each garter shut with a satisfying click. Then she'd lay out a collection of slips on her bed: delicate skeins of silk and lace, too precious for me to touch. "Which one should I wear tonight?" she'd ask, holding them up against her body. She had lovely, luscious curves and hollows in all the right places. God had given her a body most women would die for, and then He turned around and gave her a face to match.

It wasn't fair, I sometimes thought, surveying my own knobby body and desperately hunting for cheekbones. Why should she have so much and I so little—just a blaze of red hair that now and then looked pretty in the sunlight? But when my mother tried on her slips for me, all my longing was forgotten. I just stood in awe of her, so proud that such beauty ran somewhere through my own blood.

But the best part was when my mother got dressed for work. I didn't usually get to see her then, because she left the house by six a.m. But I was frequently plagued by insomnia, and I'd slip into her bedroom with the dawn and watch her in the mirror, eagerly waiting for the crisply starched, immaculate white uniform and cap that transformed her into Florence Nightingale. She worked at a big blood bank in Skid Row LA. I couldn't imagine what she did down there, amongst the homeless and tormented. Floated above them, no doubt, like the angel of mercy she was.

Everywhere, that is, except in our house.

"I take care of sick people all day long," she'd snap if I came home with the sniffles. "Do you expect me to do it here too?"

For a nurse, she had surprisingly little patience with imperfection. Once when she came home rather later than usual, I noticed a stain on her apron and made the mistake of pointing it out. Right in the middle of serving the spaghetti, she ripped the whole thing off and flung it in the trash. "Filthy mess!" she said as she kicked it away. I wasn't sure, but I got the impression she wasn't referring only to the apron.

I rolled out of bed and grabbed my favorite flannel robe, the short one with the big yellow daisies. It wasn't quite warm enough for December, but it was a gift from Daddy, and I loved it so much it was worth the shivers. I glanced again at the clock: ten minutes past five, which meant that my mother would be in her bedroom, getting ready for work. I tiptoed past her room, past the bathroom, to the kitchen. I couldn't risk turning on a light, so I fumbled around in the spice rack until I found what I was looking for: the economy-sized box of black pepper. Steeling myself for the bite, I sprinkled some into my hand, brought it up to my nose, and sniffed hard.

Wham! A firebolt erupted inside my brain, and I began to sneeze convulsively—ten, twelve, fourteen times in a row.

Before the spasm could quiet down, I ran back down the hallway and knocked on my mother's door.

"It's me," I said in broken gasps.

"What do you want? I'm getting ready."

"I'm sick," I said, letting loose a volley of sneezes for emphasis.

I could hear her exasperated sigh all the way through the door. She opened it up and stood there, one hand on her hip. "What is it?"

I couldn't really blame her. I was sick a lot, sometimes genuinely so, with a bad case of asthma and allergies, but more often than not with the pepper-induced kind. I knew how to hold the thermometer up to the lightbulb just long enough to fake a credible fever. I knew that sticking my fingers down my throat would make me throw up eventually. A swipe of my mother's taupe eye shadow underneath my eyes created a convincing pallor. All good tricks that a lot of kids knew, but the right attitude was key: listless and lethargic, so bone-numbingly weary that the only proper place for me clearly was bed.

If you had asked me, I think I would have been hard-pressed to explain why I pretended to be sick so much. I loved my classmates, loved my teachers, loved the church. Just two weeks before, I'd been elected class president—surely St. Madeleine's was the best school in the whole wide world. And I loved my parents, like a good child should: my father, who had never said no to me yet; and my mother, whom I sometimes confused with the Virgin Mary when she came to kiss me good night. I even loved my brother, although Zach lorded his three years' seniority over me and kicked me under the table when no one was looking.

But all these wonderful things meant nothing to me when the Black Beast came to call. On really bad days, he stole my eyes from me, so when I looked at my mother's prized pink geraniums, all I saw were the unpicked weeds. I saw the small strip of peeling paint on the garage and the dent on the Comet's fender. What I saw when I looked at myself was so frightful that I refused to look in the mirror. I even covered my spoon with my napkin, for fear I might catch a glimpse.

I couldn't go to school then, of course. Everyone expected so much of me there: the teachers, the students, the priest. I was supposed to be the first one waving my hand in the air with the answer, but I could barely hold it up long enough to brush my teeth. Everything felt so heavy then: my arms, my legs, my heart. My friends wanted mischief and magic from me. I was the schoolyard sprite, the instigator of all grand recess schemes. No one wanted to hear how much it hurt just to smile, how hard it was to nod and pretend that I was listening to anything other than my own private howl. Or at least that's what I assumed. I never risked the attempt. It was easier—safer, far wiser, no doubt—just to stay home, curl up in bed, and read. Bed asked nothing of me but inertia, which was all that I could deliver.

Worst of all, when the Black Beast was in this kind of mood, I couldn't do the one thing that made life truly meaningful for me: I couldn't snuggle up with my father in his big brown chair and read the evening paper. Daddy came home late at night, but it didn't matter. He always found time to read to me, to explain who Robert F. Kennedy was, what the fight for civil rights was all about, and why the Beatles mattered. For dessert, he'd turn to the funny pages and make sure that I got every joke.

But the Black Beast would do something strange to my sense of smell, so that my father's beloved aroma of unfiltered Camels and aftershave suddenly seemed noxious to me. It was easier just to plead sickness and go straight off to bed than to risk insulting him with my upturned nose. Plus I couldn't seem to muster the exuberance required to scramble into his chair and bombard him with pertinent questions. Sustained interest in anything beside myself was practically impossible.

I slipped past my mother and sidled up next to her bureau. My timing was perfect—she was just about to take her pill. I watched as she uncapped the bottle, shook the tiny blue pill out onto her hand, then swallowed it with a sip of water. I imagined it traveling down the swan's length of her throat, and I wondered if I'd look anywhere near as graceful when I downed the entire bottle.

She placed the bottle back in the drawer, then bent down to lace up her shiny white shoes. As soon as her back was turned, I rummaged around in her lingerie until, at last, I found it. I stuffed the bottle deep into my pocket and swung back around to face her, innocence engraved across my face. She was still tugging on her laces. So far as I could tell, she hadn't seen a thing.

Now that I had the pills in my possession, I was eager to leave. Faking a couple more sneezes, I told my mother I felt dizzy and needed to go back to bed. She looked at me suspiciously. "What do you do there all day in bed?"

I blinked. What did she mean? What did she know? I never really thought that she'd noticed how much time I spent in bed—she was so busy working and making dinner and arguing with Daddy. I felt strangely violated somehow, as if I were being spied on in my undies. I decided to bluff, to play it cool.

"I read," I said. "I rest. Sometimes I say the rosary."

She frowned. "I don't know why we pay all that fancy tuition if you're never going to be in school."

I'd heard this argument before, and a whine crept into my voice. "But Mom, I'm really sick."

She ignored me. "Tonight, no matter what, we're going to fix that hem. I won't have you parading around in public looking like a ragamuffin."

I suddenly felt genuinely ill. She was referring to my First Communion dress, the lovely white froth in my closet, the hem of which had come partially undone. It was the most beautiful thing I'd ever seen, except of course for my mother. The big Mass was scheduled for this coming Sunday, five days away. And because I was the class president, I was certain that I would lead the procession up to the altar. Every eye in the church would be on me, which was surely how God intended things, except—

Except that if all went well, I would be dead by then.

It wasn't fair. I'd tried on that dress so many times I knew every seam by heart. I had a makeshift altar in the corner of my room, and I'd practiced in front of it dozens of times: the graceful walk up the center aisle, eyes demurely downcast, face aglow with anticipation. Then I'd sink to my knees and tilt my head back, my mouth slightly open, eager for God to enter me through His sacred host. Somewhere I had picked up the notion that a girl at her First Communion was like the bride of Christ. True or not, I felt as tingly as if I were waiting for my very first kiss.

The biggest moment of my life, and I was going to miss it.

I walked back slowly to my room and sank down on my bed. The blank white construction paper taunted me from across the room. Maybe, just maybe, my writing skills were good enough. Maybe if I used a ruler, the lines would be sufficiently straight, and no one would notice it was the wrong kind of paper . . .

But what to write? I'd been so worried about my printing that I'd never even thought of the bigger problem: I was supposed to tell a story about myself. It would have to be so deeply engrossing that Sister Mary Bernadette would ignore the less than perfect lettering and feel compelled to give it a rousing A-plus. But look at my life: nothing ever happened to me. I got up, made my bed, had breakfast, went to school, came home, watched TV, ate dinner, went to bed. Fish on Friday, church on Sunday, dance class on Tuesday afternoons. Day after day, week after week, the same routine over and over again. The only thing of any interest in my life was the Black Beast, and of course, I couldn't write about that. I'd be kicked out of St. Madeleine's for good.

I curled up into a little ball, drawing my knees so tight against my chest that I could feel the outline of the pill bottle against my thigh. Just then I heard my mother's footsteps in the hall. "I'm leaving!" she yelled.

"I'm asleep!" I yelled back, not realizing until I said it how silly that was. But the only answer I received was the sound of the front door slamming shut.

In spite of all the noise, my father still slept soundly in the guest room. He'd been sleeping in the guest room for as long as I could remember. My mother claimed he snored; he vehemently denied it. It was my job to wake him up so he could fix breakfast and take Zach and me to school. It wasn't easy: my father could sleep through an earthquake (and had, several times). He told me once that World War II had taught him how to sleep through anything.

It wasn't quite time to wake him yet, so I decided to take a few minutes and figure out what to wear for the big event. I surveyed my closet: black seemed like the obvious choice. Then they wouldn't even have to change me for the funeral. But my mother didn't like how I looked in black, so the only thing I owned in that color was my witch's costume from last Halloween. I worried how that might look to God—as if I were courting the devil. There was my Pop Warner cheerleading outfit, but the skirt had grown rather short this past year, and that didn't seem very dignified. In fact, it seemed like I'd outgrown almost all my good outfits. Except—of course!—my First Communion dress.

I took it off the hanger and laid it out on the bed, taking care not to snag the loose hem. It was just the right white, like a freshly washed soul. Real lace covered the entire bodice, and there was a scratchy petticoat underneath that made the skirt stand out stiffly from my body. I loved the slight discomfort against my skin. It was my very own version of a hair shirt—it made me feel as if I were doing penance.

And then there was the veil. I spread it out carefully next to the dress; a long length of gossamer fabric. I'd wheedled my mother into buying me the biggest one the store had in stock, even though she kept insisting it was too dramatic. I knew it wasn't. Somehow, at seven, I already knew the effect that exaggeration could have on an audience. I'd had to use it often enough, so that the Black Beast could get his own way.

But of course, no one was going to see it on me now. My exhilaration began to deflate, until I realized that the veil would make a perfect shroud. I'd wrap it around and around my body, just like Mary Magdalene had wrapped Jesus's body when she'd taken him down from the Cross. I'd die in white, like a true bride of Christ.

That settled, I went to wake Daddy. His room, unlike my mother's, was never locked. I went in and out as much as I liked, played with his cuff links, pawed through his dresser drawers. A few of my stuffed animals even lived on his pillow, next to his sleeping head. One of his arms lay outside the covers, and I gave it a gentle shake.

"Daddy, it's time," I said. Nothing. I tried again. Not a flicker. I jumped on the bed and gave his arm a serious yank, just like in tug-of-war. His eyes popped open. "What the hell?" he said.

Daddy was allowed to swear because he wasn't Catholic. He wasn't quite sure what he was, and he didn't seem to care. I thought that was the coolest thing in the world because it meant he didn't have to follow the rules. He didn't have to eat smelly fish on Fridays, he didn't have to go to confession, he didn't even have to kneel during Mass. While the rest of us bruised our tender knees, he sat back with impunity. Once or twice, I looked over my shoulder at him, and I could swear I caught him grinning.

"It's morning!" I said, tickling him in the ribs.

"Obviously," he grunted, and rolled on his side. "Go away, you miserable child."

I knew my father well enough to ignore his moment of pique. I could count on one hand the number of times he'd been seriously angry with me. But that didn't mean he didn't have a temper. It was terrifying, like a lightning storm in summer: just as sudden and just as short-lived. He'd flare up at my mother with a big, booming voice, his face bright red, the veins bulging out of his forehead. Then the next minute, his eyes would grow quiet again, soft and brown, like my bedtime cocoa.

I tickled him again. This time his hand shot up and grabbed me by the wrist, then he pulled me down next to him and tickled me until I collapsed with laughter. "Who's the lazybones now?" he said. "Come on, last one up's a soggy pancake."

I ran to the kitchen, but his legs were longer than mine, and he beat me. Ours was a well-oiled machine by now: I would gather up all the pancake ingredients while he coaxed the old griddle to life. By the time it was hot, I'd have everything waiting: Bisquick mix, eggs, milk, maple syrup. There was an annoying interruption every morning while my father fixed himself a cup of coffee. That morning, I didn't want to delay even a minute before we played the pancake game—especially since it would be the last time I ever played it on this earth.

The game was simple and dated back to the time when I was

first learning how to read. Daddy would drizzle the batter into letters, and I wasn't allowed to eat until I knew which letter was represented. My favorite was *T* for "Terri," of course, but I also liked *J* for "Jack." Now that I had learned my alphabet, the game had progressed so that I had to spell ten words that began with the letter before I could dive into my pancakes. Not little words, like *go* or *get*, but big words, like *geranium* and *geography*. "Next week," my father informed me, pouring out the batter, "we're going to do proper names from history." That was okay, I thought, drowning my new batch with maple syrup. I didn't mind cold pancakes.

"Where is your brother this morning?" my father asked, sitting down with his coffee. It was as much a part of our routine as the recalcitrant griddle.

"Don't know," I said, which wasn't the truth. I knew. My father knew. My mother knew. We all knew. Zach was in his room. Zach was always in his room. What he did there, with his towering stacks of *National Geographic*s and his enormous collection of cap guns, we had no clue. We were never invited in. I, particularly, was forbidden to enter. I think I must have offended Zach deeply just by virtue of my entry into his world. It couldn't have been easy for him, as firstborn and sole possessor of the stage, to have the spotlight yanked away by a red-faced, squalling infant. In his defense, I must admit I really can't blame him: from the day that I came into this world, I did everything in my power to keep that spotlight trained on me.

My mother often argued with my father about this disparity of attention. "Jack, you're spoiling her rotten," she'd say. "And it's completely unfair to Zach." No doubt she was right. It wasn't fair. But I wasn't in the business of fairness, I was in the business of staking my territory. The world did not feel safe to me, and between my father and mother, my father seemed the more likely refuge from harm. Not that I didn't love my mother, but I knew those pink geraniums in front of our house bloomed only so long as she was happy, and her happiness seemed a precarious thing, entirely dependent on mysterious words like *mortgage* and *Rebecca*.

But except for his occasional outbursts of temper, my father was uniformly easygoing, charming, and relaxed. He seemed to me to have things in hand. Best of all, he thought I was adorable: the smartest, the cleverest, the most competent child ever invented. And he told me so constantly. The most effusive my mother ever got was, "Button your sweater, it's chilly outside."

I never meant my bond with my father to get in the way of his relationship with Zach. But a child's soul is inherently selfish, and in truth, I was pleased to have so much of my father's time to myself. The way I saw it, Daddy's love was the ultimate A-plus, and Zach was doing nothing to earn it by hiding away in his room all day. Whereas my campaign never ceased.

I'd set up my station by his big brown chair a half hour before he got home. In one pile was all my schoolwork, including any excellent grades or comments or honors I'd won that day. In another, the *Daily Report*, folded just the way he liked it. In a third, the amenities: cigarettes, lighter, the ashtray I made for him in kindergarten, his bedroom slippers, and his favorite heavy-bottomed scotch glass. The one thing my mother refused to let me do was fill up the glass ahead of time. "He can fix his own damned drink," she'd say. She, as a Catholic, was not permitted profanity, so her use of it impressed me. Alcohol quickly became associated in my mind with a flagrant disregard for the rules.

Then I would wait by the door. I hated that door. No, I loved it. It was the door my father would enter from, and that, of course, made it perfect. But it was also the door that he would slam on his way out of the house after one of their endless late-night arguments. I'd be lying in bed, just waiting for it, but nothing ever prepared me for the awful sound of that slam. The whole house would reverberate with it, but I would continue to shake long after the house settled down.

I knew that he would leave one day. It was a fact of my existence, as glaring as my strawberry hair. It was the central mission of my life to make sure that when he left, he took me with him. Which was why I simply couldn't risk coming home with a C on this latest homework assignment. Things had been tenser than usual lately. A week ago, Daddy had slammed the door and hadn't come home for two days.

"He's working," my mother had said when I'd begged to know where he was. But I knew that couldn't be true. He was working on a nearby tract of homes, and he'd never had to leave before. Besides, he would have told me if he was going anywhere. We would have looked it up together on the map, he would have given me ten proper names to spell, there would have been a quiz on it later. So she must have been lying, and I could feel the earth begin to shift ever so slightly but treacherously beneath my feet. Now was clearly not the time to loosen my hold.

There was a flaw to my logic, of course. If I killed myself to avoid losing my father, I'd be dead, and I'd lose him forever. "Forever" wasn't quite clear to me. Forever could be an afternoon if the Black Beast was impatient that day, or it could be a lifetime. At six, I didn't have much of a grasp of finality. I just knew that forever sounded like a long, long time to be without my daddy.

The only way out of this conundrum was faith. I simply had to believe with all my heart and soul in what Sister Mary Bernadette had taught us about the nature of Heaven: that the moment you reach the Pearly Gates, everyone you ever loved, dead or alive, is gathered around to meet you. She assured us that this included dead pets and lost stuffed animals, so it had to apply to beloved fathers too. Please, sweet Jesus, make it so.

"Why are your eyes closed?" my father asked. I was startled — prayer had just snuck up on me; I hadn't meant for him to see it.

"I'm sleepy," I started to answer, and then I remembered that I needed him to call the school for me, to get me excused for the day. "No, you know what? I'm sick. I woke up this morning with a terrible cold. You should have heard me sneezing. Mom was really worried."

"Did she say that I should call the school?"

I hesitated, not wanting to burden my soul with another lie so close to my death. "I'm sure she just assumed you would. She was in an awful hurry." That much, at least, was true.

My mother's opinion as to matters of physical health was

absolute and final. Anyone seeing her in her shining white uniform would have followed her instructions to the letter. "Hand me the phone," my father said.

While he dialed, I studied his face: the high curving forehead, the broad Cheney nose, the endearing gap between his two front teeth, the wayward lock of sandy brown hair. I wanted to commit every detail to memory. I'd never gone anywhere without my daddy before, and death was the longest journey of all. Sure, I believed he'd be there to greet me in Heaven, but who knew how long it would take me to arrive? Even Disneyland had lines; maybe Heaven did too.

A flutter of emotions kicked up inside me: fear, doubt, loneliness, regret. For all his years of single-minded devotion, I felt I owed my father something. An explanation, perhaps. At the very least, a good-bye. Trembling, I opened my mouth to speak—and Zach walked into the kitchen.

"Where's breakfast?" he asked, slinging his book bag onto the counter and pulling up a chair as best he could with his bandaged hand. I avoided looking at it.

"We already ate. Get it yourself." I didn't mean to snap, but his timing was lousy.

"What's with you? And why aren't you dressed?" He got up and clumsily poured himself a heaping bowl of raisin bran.

"I'm sick," I said.

He snorted. "Again? What is it this time? Lung cancer?"

My father hung up the phone. "Okay, you're all set. But Anna Marie can't come for an hour. Will you be all right until then?"

I nodded. Since they both worked, my parents were sometimes forced to leave us alone for short periods of time. It was
no big deal. We lived on a quiet cul-de-sac, and the neighbors
all kept an eye out for one another. It seemed unlikely that
anything bad could ever happen in our peaceful, middle-class
neighborhood, with its neatly trimmed hedges and meticulous
flower beds.

Anna Marie was the girl down the street who came and sat
with Zach and me after school until my mother got home. *Sat*
was literally all she did. She parked her hefty carcass on the sofa
and watched TV while simultaneously eating potato chips and
flipping through the latest teen magazine. Zach was in his room,
of course, so she had nothing to do with him. Once or twice, I'd
tried to befriend her, but short of discovering that we both liked
extra salt on our potato chips, I couldn't find much in common.
So Anna Marie wouldn't hinder my plans. She barely even noticed that I was alive; I doubt that she'd know I was dead.

"I'm halfway through *Misty of Chincoteague*," I reassured
my father. "Plus I've got an overdue homework assignment." I
regretted the words as soon as I spoke them.

My father's face turned serious. "What's this?"

"You know. I'm supposed to write a story about myself."

"And?"

"I can't think what I should write."

"Write about anything. Write about—" His eye caught the
vase on the dining room table. "Flowers. Say what kind of flower
you are."

"Okay." I shrugged. What did it matter now, anyway?

"Come on, Zach, we're late," my father said.

Zach stayed in his seat, frowning. "My hand hurts. And I think I'm getting a sore throat. I should be able to stay home too."

"Forget it," my father said.

"Why is she the only one who gets to lounge around all day?"

"Because she's not the one who just got a D-minus on a math test. Out with you."

My father scooped up his keys off the counter and held out his arms. "Give us a kiss, princess." Knowing this would be the very last kiss nearly undid me. I hurled myself into my father's arms and hugged his waist so tight I could feel his belt cutting into my skin. Then I burst into tears.

"Whoa, what's this?" He stroked my hair. "You're not afraid to stay home alone now, are you? A big girl like you?"

I didn't want him to remember me like this. I'm not sure I knew the exact words yet, but I wanted him to remember my dignity. Grace. Poise. "No, of course not," I said, shaking my hair back out of my face and cracking a lopsided smile.

"That's better. Give 'em hell, baby." It was his signature line, the one he always said before we had to part. As always, it stiffened my spine and made me feel like a soldier on my way to the wars.

"Bye, Daddy," I said softly to his retreating back. Zach sped by me, saying, "Don't cough up any blood on the couches. Mom'll kill you."

"Bye-bye, Zach," I said with far more tenderness than I had ever mustered toward him before.

And then they were gone, and the house was all mine. My footsteps echoed on the hardwood floors. I caught a glimpse of myself in the living room mirror and decided not to look in mirrors anymore. I looked far too small for the big deed that I needed to do.

I thought about preparing one last grand meal, full of everything I was usually denied: chocolate chip cookie dough, a great big root beer float, Cheetos, corn chips, and an economy-sized bag of M&M's for dessert. But I just wasn't hungry. There were things to do, and Anna Marie was coming in an hour. If I was going on this journey, I needed to pack. I realized that packing for the afterlife might be futile, but those mummies had been pretty smart, and they had brought along a thing or two.

I had my very own suitcase: a small pink one that my mother had bought me when we visited her family's farm in Canada a few years before. Standing on a kitchen chair, I wrestled it down from the closet shelf. It was empty except for one photograph tucked away in one of the silk-lined compartments. I remembered that photograph, although I wished that I didn't. It showed what appeared to be a wild child, a seething mass of hair and bared teeth. Her mouth was open, clearly screaming. The child was locked in an empty cage.

The Black Beast had been upon me then. I'd been bad: I hadn't wanted to go to a livestock show with the rest of my cousins. I hadn't wanted to do anything, just wallow in bed. But I was maybe four or five, and of course, they couldn't leave me behind. One of my cousins joked, "Let's put her in the cage" — the one they used to carry the pigs. They tossed me in there and locked the door. It was a sweltering day, and the smell of shit was so thick and strong I thought I'd suffocate. Flies swarmed all around me, buzzing angrily in my ears and crawling in my eyes, my nose.

The Black Beast went berserk. I didn't know any swear words then, I only knew how to scream. And scream I did, so loudly and so long that I lost the use of my voice for days after.

It was the first time I remembered ever losing control. In spite of my fury, in spite of my righteous indignation, the abandon felt delicious. It was like I lived on a freer, wilder plane than my grubby, earth-bound cousins, who by now were gathered around laughing, snapping photos of me. I played to the camera, loping around like a crazed gorilla, beating my chest, banging my head against the bars. I lost myself entirely in the part, leaving behind the immaculately dressed little girl in her polka-dot socks and Mary Jane shoes. I scooped up some dirt (mixed with pig dung, no doubt) and smeared it across my face, my dress. I was just about to start eating it when my aunt caught sight of us from the farmhouse window and made my cousins release me.

I got a lot of attention after that: a warm bubble bath, an extra helping of my Aunt Dolores's famous mashed potatoes, and the right to keep the light on if I wanted. My dreams were full of cages from that night on.

I slipped the photograph back in its place and lugged the suitcase into my room. What to pack? Daddy had read me an article once about King Tut, the boy king who'd been buried with his gold. I had no gold, but I did have a genuine pearl pinkie ring from SeaWorld. In it went. There wasn't much else in the way of treasure, so I just took what was most precious to me. Toto, of course; maybe God could restore his missing ear. An old picture of my mother with her arm around my father's waist—it was one of the few times I'd seen them embrace. All seven books of *The Chronicles of Narnia*. (I left the lives of the saints behind, figuring that I could interview them in person.) But I didn't take a single honor or award. There were lots of them lining my bookshelf: plaques and trophies and parchment scrolls. The best of this. Most valued that. In Heaven, I was sure, none of this would matter.

I shook my head in wonder. Imagine: a world without grades, without prizes. How would God know that I was the best? Would He still love me anyway?

I shut the suitcase and snapped it closed. The house was quiet. I could hear the clock out in the hall. I could hear the leaky faucet in my mother's bath, the one she kept nagging my father to fix. Our house abutted the freeway, and the sound of the traffic was sometimes so loud it made conversation difficult. But it was strangely muted that day, as if all the cars were running on velvet. The world was hushed and waiting.

I sat on the bed and pulled the pill bottle out of my pocket. I tried to read the label, but it was an unintelligible mass of mostly vowels, followed by "Take as directed." It didn't really matter what they were called, I supposed. Everyone knew that pills were dangerous; that's why they hid them in the lingerie drawer or on the very top shelf of the medicine cabinet.

I went in the bathroom and filled my toothpaste glass with cold water. Then I opened the bottle and emptied it out on my bedspread. Damn. There weren't nearly as many as I'd hoped there would be: twenty-five—no, twenty-six—little blue pills. Was that enough to do the trick? Or would I end up a vegetable like my mother's great-aunt Rosemarie, with the perpetual spittle in the corners of her mouth that nobody bothered to wipe away?

One thing was for sure: I couldn't do this alone. I pulled Toto out of the suitcase and held him tight, careful not to crush his ear. Then I knelt down on the floor and prayed for guidance: "Dear God, I'm sorry if this is a sin, but please don't let me mess it up."

Not a very eloquent prayer, but deeply sincere. I got up, slipped off the robe with the big yellow daisies, and packed it carefully in the suitcase. Then I put on my First Communion dress—or rather, I tried to put it on. There was a row of little pearl-covered buttons in the back, which I couldn't quite manage by myself. I felt an intense and sudden longing for my mother, with her efficient, nimble fingers. It was not the most auspicious start, to arrive at Heaven half-buttoned.

I checked the clock. Eight-thirty, and Anna Marie would be here at nine. If I was ever going to do this, now was the time. Now, now, now, the Black Beast commanded.

All at once, I felt a curious sensation, as if my body had split in two and was watching itself. I observed my right hand reach out and pick up one of the little blue pills. It was strange: I wasn't afraid. In fact, if I had known the word, I think I would have said I felt serene: the decision had finally been made. But

I noticed that my hand was shaking, and my fingers were icy white. I placed the pill on the tip of my tongue and waited, tasting. It was bitter; so bitter it made my eyes squint. I took a long, cool drink of water and felt it course down the back of my throat, sweeping the pill along with it.

Now it was just like homework: I simply had to dive in and finish. I attacked the pills like potato chips. Over and over, I picked one up, placed it on my tongue, took a sip of water, and swallowed, until they were all gone. Around about the seventh pill, I noticed that my hand was still shaking. But other than that, I felt no different. I saw no visions, I heard no trumpets. Death tasted familiar, like toothpaste.

This wasn't what I'd expected. I'd thought the pills would kill me instantly, and I'd be whooshed straight into Heaven, like in *The Wizard of Oz* when Dorothy is swept out of black-and-white into glowing Technicolor. But I looked around, and the room was unchanged. Same old macramé wall hanging, same old faded pink sheets. I looked under the bed. Same old dust bunnies too.

I was pretty sure I knew why I was still here. God didn't want to take me yet because my homework wasn't finished. Reluctantly, I got out of bed and walked over to my desk. I contemplated the horrid white paper. It looked even whiter and blanker than I'd remembered it. Write a story about yourself, Sister Mary Bernadette had said. I'd halfway promised my father at breakfast that I would—a story about flowers, I think he had said. What kind of flower was I?

My left temple was pulsing, and I felt slightly woozy, but I forced myself to sit down and face the page. The assignment seemed absurd to me. If I'd known what kind of flower I was, no doubt I wouldn't be in this predicament. I'd be happy, in the right kind of garden, content just to be a daisy. But all I knew, all I'd ever known, was what I was not.

I grabbed my favorite crayon, burnt sienna, and started writing:

I'm not a rose like St. Thérèse
Or a lily like Joan of Arc
But a—

Here I stopped. I knew the image I wanted, but my mind was beginning to slip sideways and I couldn't remember the name of the flower. It was shy and grew between the cracks—probably the last thing anyone would ever expect me to say about myself, but with death on my shoulder, I felt compelled to tell the truth. That was me, that little yellow flower always about to be crushed underfoot.

A sudden wave of nausea struck me, and I ran to the bathroom and was promptly sick. Plus I'd never had to pee so badly in my life. Once I did, the nausea lifted somewhat, and I made my way back to the desk. My legs felt as if they belonged to someone else, but my hands still worked, although the trembling was worse than ever. I examined what I'd written. Sure enough, it was wildly imperfect, the printing scrawled all over the page. I wanted to cry, but I was too preoccupied by the sensations erupting in my body: dizziness, thirst, and a violent buzzing in my ears. The paper was growing whiter by the second, the room began to spin and throb, and I barely made it back to my bed before I knew no more.

I woke to discover that Heaven looked just like my mother's eyes. They were enormous; they filled the whole universe.

"You were sleeping so soundly, I didn't want to wake you," she said. "Anna Marie told me you were out like a light all afternoon."

I hadn't really expected to see my mother in Heaven. I thought she'd be so mad at me for stealing her pills, she'd never want to see me again. But here she was, and her voice was so soothing—soft and low and vibrant with concern—that I knew all must be forgiven. The whiteness of her uniform dazzled me. Clearly, she was an angel, and I'd never done her justice before.

I held out my arms to embrace her, but the motion unnerved me and I threw up all over the pillow. With one swift yank, she pulled off the pillowcase before it could soil the sheets. Then she kicked into nursing mode, laying one cool hand across my forehead, checking my pulse with the other. I loved it when my mother checked my pulse: she didn't often touch me, and it felt like she was sending filaments of empathy straight through my wrist.

I leaned in to kiss her. She pulled back, let go of my wrist, and wrinkled her nose. "You'd better go brush your teeth," she said. "And get out of that dress so I can fix the hem. I won't have people saying I neglect my children."

Shaky and dizzy, I went into the bathroom. I had a tremendous urge to pee again, but as I sat down, it occurred to me: there shouldn't be toilets in Heaven. Nor should my mother pull away from my kiss. I realized then that I had failed—I had not scored an A-plus at suicide. What was I going to do now? I felt a sudden wetness on my cheeks, but I didn't even look in the mirror to confirm that I was crying. I knew what I would see there: eyes like dead coals. I took off my dress and crawled into bed, careful not to let my mother see me cry.

"Dinner's at six," she said.

"I'm not hungry."

"Suit yourself," she shrugged. "It's corn dogs." She knew that was one of my favorite meals, but the prospect of food didn't appeal to me. The thought of getting up and getting dressed was just too much to handle. I nestled Toto against my cheek and let him sop up my tears.

Sleep consumed me, and cages haunted my dreams. I was trapped and in danger, and there was no getting out. At some point, I thought I heard a man's voice—my father's, perhaps?—and felt familiar lips brushing my forehead. But it didn't matter. The cages only grew smaller and tighter, the locks more cruelly intricate.

When I woke the next morning, I was seven.

I felt a burning thirst and that same insatiable need to pee. On my way out of the bathroom, I ran into my mother. She looked harried. "Have you seen my pills?" she asked.

"What pills?" I smoothed my face into a blank.

"You know, those little blue pills I take every morning. My diuretics."

"Your what?"

"My diuretics. My ankles are going to swell like elephants' legs if I can't find them. Come help me look."

"I don't know where you keep them."

"In my lingerie drawer. Mind you don't mess it up. And hurry."

It was impossible to hurry. My arms and legs felt like sacks of bricks and didn't want to move. I spent the next ten minutes pretending to look for what I already knew wasn't there. I'd hidden the bottle in a shoe box in the very back of my closet. There was no chance of it ever coming to light. But I sifted and sorted most diligently while my mother tore the rest of the room apart. Naturally, she found nothing.

"This means I'll have to wear support hose today," she said finally. "I can't stand support hose. I don't even know where they are. I hate this stupid house, where you can never find anything."

I felt a little guilty then, but not enough to tell her my secret. Besides, the Black Beast had hold of my tongue, and it was difficult to speak. I wanted to say, "Don't you even realize that I'm seven today?" but there were too many syllables in that sentence and too much emotion required to voice them. I left my mother ransacking her drawers and burrowed back under the covers.

Seventh birthdays are highly overrated. I slept almost the entire day. I didn't have to resort to the pepper trick or stick a thermometer under my arm. Nobody expected me to go to school. My mother had left a note, so my father didn't even try to wake me. He told Anna Marie to give me two aspirins when I woke up, but I never did. "I tried to call you all day, but you were asleep, and your mother thought it best that we leave you be," he told me later that evening. I guess I must have looked as sick as I felt.

I was still a bit queasy from all the pills, but of course, that wasn't the problem. It was the Black Beast, sitting on my chest. Each and every one of my bones felt too heavy for my body. Blinking and breathing, no longer automatic functions, had turned into strenuous acts of will. It was all I could do just to pull in my ribs and push them back out again, over and over. And always, behind each labored breath, was the knowledge that I had failed. Like it or not, I was going to live.

There was a cake—a fancy one, with ballerinas pirouetting all over it. Chocolate with buttercream icing, my favorite. While everyone sang the birthday song, I closed my eyes and pretended to make a wish. But there was only one thing to wish for, and I think I had already exhausted it: "Please don't let me get a C."

I even got the presents I wanted most: an Easy-Bake Oven and a beautiful hand-tooled red leather diary with its very own lock and key. I was a creature of secret thoughts; now I had somewhere to put them. I forced a smile and tried to sound gay, but it came out rather lugubrious.

"You're still not feeling well, are you?" my father asked.

I shook my head.

"Do you feel too sick to go to school tomorrow?"

I nodded, hard.

"Jack, she's already been out almost ten days," my mother said. "You're indulging her, as always. And don't forget, her First Communion's on Sunday."

That was three days away. "The only thing she really needs to show up for is confession on Saturday," my father argued. "She'll be good and rested by then. Won't you, princess?"

I threw my arms around his neck. "I'll sleep all day, I promise."

My mother shot him a look of disgust, but he got on the phone to Anna Marie. "Terri Lynn's having one of her spells," he said. "We'll need you tomorrow and Friday, okay?"

"One of her spells." I'd often heard my parents use that phrase, but I wasn't quite sure what it meant. Was I simply being ungovernable? Or was it possible, however unlikely, that they knew about the Black Beast? I immediately dismissed that notion. No one had ever mentioned it, and ours was too small a household for diplomacy.

Anna Marie was available, so I was all set. I'd rest up Thursday and Friday and go to confession on Saturday. Confession was, of course, mandatory before a First Communion. All sins must be cleansed, all impurities banished, before one could receive the body of Christ. I'd have an awful lot of confessing to do, I realized. I dreaded to think what Father Joseph would say, or what kind of penance he'd give me for attempting suicide—that most mortal of mortal sins.

I worried about it the whole next day, and the whole day Friday too. That's all I did: worry, lie in bed, and eat myself into a stupor. As always, I went for anything sweet: apricot jam and Oreo cookies, chocolate chip ice cream drenched in pancake syrup, powdered sugar straight out of the box. My face and hair were covered with sugar, my precious robe spattered with chocolate, but I just kept shoveling it in—I couldn't stop. Anna Marie didn't care what I ate. She even helped me polish off the rest of the birthday cake.

When everything obvious was consumed, I grabbed the box of raisin bran and picked out all the raisins. They tasted all the sweeter when I imagined Zach's face in the morning.

"Dad, she's done it again," he'd say, when he poured out his favorite cereal.

My father would look sympathetic and shrug. No matter how many times they ordered me not to vandalize the raisin bran, the Black Beast wouldn't let it alone. It amused him too much to antagonize Zach—a dangerous game, I thought.

When I woke up Saturday morning, it was raining so hard that I was certain I'd been granted a reprieve. Surely no one would expect the students to go to confession in a torrent like this. But my father called the convent, and it was confirmed: if I didn't go to confession, there would be no First Communion for me tomorrow.

Southern California so rarely has weather, the thunder and lightning would have been thrilling if it had been just any old day. But that day, the storm seemed like proof of God's displeasure with me, rattling my eardrums and stinging my skin. We had to drive so slowly on the slick, flooded roads that the trip to St. Madeleine's took forever, and we passed a bad accident on

the way. I was thoroughly frightened and miserable by the time
we reached the church. Despite my entreaties, my father stayed
in the car to smoke a Camel. "Give 'em hell, baby," he said.

Father Joseph had apparently been caught in the rain. His
cassock was so wet it was streaming, leaving a dark trail behind
him. The soaking hadn't helped his disposition either, which
even on the best of days was dour. "Line up!" he barked at the
twenty or so shivering students waiting to confess. "No talking!
No fidgeting! Contemplate your sins!" Probably none of us
knew what "contemplate" meant, but like puppies listening to a
master's tone, we knew enough to stay quiet.

I was one of the first in line, which was good because it
meant I didn't have too much time to think. The light over the
confessional went off, and Johnny Zinn stepped out. He was the
toughest kid in class, and he was in tears. "Next!" Father Joseph
shouted.

I stepped in, knelt, and crossed myself. It was dark and dank
and close in there, the air a mixture of Johnny Zinn's sweat and
the incense lingering from the morning Mass. My body tem-
perature began to rise, my heart began to flutter. As always, I
worried that I would faint before Father Joseph could speak to
me. I could hear him breathing through the screen; it sounded
like he had a bad cold. Then he shot the secret panel back and
said something in Latin. My cue.

"Bless me, Father, for I have sinned. It has been three weeks
since my last confession, and these are my sins."

I'd already decided that I wouldn't use the word *suicide*.
Instead I would just state the facts and let Father Joseph come

to his own conclusion. It wasn't really a lie that way, just a soft-ening of the truth. I took a deep breath and said, "I stole my mother's diabetics." Then I added in a rush, "And I took them all." There, I'd said it. The ball was in God's court now.

I expected Father Joseph to be outraged. At the very least, I thought he'd ask me why I did it and then lecture me on the peril to my mortal soul. But there was silence on the other side of the panel, followed by a very great sneeze and a copious amount of nose blowing. When he finally spoke, he sounded congested and bored.

"Stealing is a serious sin," he said. I wondered how many times he had to say that in the course of a week's confessions.

"Yes, Father, I know."

"Search your heart, child. Are you truly sorry?"

I searched my heart, but the truth was, my only real regret was that I hadn't succeeded. So I decided to be sorry about that.

"Yes, I'm truly sorry."

"Then I absolve you, in the name of the Father, the Son, and the Holy Ghost." He assigned me penance: something like twenty Hail Marys and ten Our Fathers. Mumbling another mouthful of Latin, he bid me to "go in peace and sin no more." The panel slid shut, and I was free.

I stepped out into a newly made world. The rain had stopped, and a single ray of sunshine pierced the Annunciation stained glass window, lighting up the altar and the very first pew. A man sat there, not kneeling, not praying, but nonchalantly reading the newspaper. I rushed to him and gave him a hug.

"How'd it go, princess?"

"Perfect. What's that?" I pointed to a cardboard box at his side.

"Another little birthday present for you. While you were in there"—he jerked his thumb toward the confessional—"I stopped by the convent to see Sister Mary Bernadette. I told her how concerned you were about not having the right paper for that latest homework assignment, and she gave me this." He handed me the box.

I opened it slowly, afraid to be disappointed. But I should have trusted the setting: God's house, my father's hands, that single ray of light. It was indeed a miracle: twenty, maybe thirty pages of clean manila paper, marked across with those thin blue lines that made it so easy for me to print to perfection. I would get that A-plus after all. My father wouldn't leave me, at least not for the foreseeable future. I was so overwhelmed I sank down to my knees.

"I have to say my penance now," I said.

But instead I gave thanks: for the paper, for my father's thoughtfulness, for Sister Mary Bernadette's generosity. For the sunlight, which was now beginning to flood all the stained glass windows. For surviving yet another day, despite my fears, despite my imperfections, and despite the Black Beast.

My exaltation flickered for a moment. Who was the Black Beast, anyway, and why did he torment me so? Why did he make my moods plummet and soar, so quickly and intensely? Why did everything seem to matter so much? I looked over at Johnny Zinn, surreptitiously picking his nose in the next pew. I was sure he would never care enough about a homework assignment to want to kill himself. Why couldn't I just be a normal kid?

A shadow fell across the nave, and for a moment I shivered. But it passed, and the light that succeeded it was so brilliant, I let my dark questions be swallowed up for yet another day. I was only seven, after all. Maybe life would get simpler by the time I was eight. I decided to put off saying my penance, and reached up and tugged on my father's sleeve.

"I'm ready now," I whispered.

"That was fast," he said. "You must not have been very bad."

I didn't respond. Clutching my paper tight to my chest, I walked down the aisle, followed by the glittering eyes of saints.

2

The world is darkness, the only light
The devil's eyes, piercing my soul—
I feel no remorse, I know this is right
I sinned on earth, I must pay the toll.

—Age ten

Life did not get simpler at eight. Or at nine.

My "spells" continued, and I racked up lengthy absences from school. Although these were difficult years, they were not especially memorable. Ten was different. Ten was a watershed year, exuberant and unforgettable. Life was all around me, begging to be seen, touched, tasted, inhaled. My senses had never felt so sharp. I could smell the neighborhood cur coming from half a block away. I could suck the secrets out of my mother's oatmeal cookies, even the elusive nutmeg, with one bite. And nobody was faster at dodgeball.

Lush as it was, there were times when I regretted this acute sensibility. Late at night, a branch scratching my bedroom window was a witch's fingernail, trying to get at me. When the Santa Ana winds blew into town, my eyes glowed too bright and my skin felt like kindling, crisp and dry and ready to burn. One morning, I took a walk through our backyard, and the beauty of the bougainvillea along the pool fence proved too much for me: I lay down in the grass and sobbed.

At moments like this, my only real relief was in poetry. Everything I wrote was drenched in feeling. Despite the fact that I was so much more chipper at ten, a shocking percentage of my early writing was about death and dying and, as one title so aptly put it, "The Gloom Everlasting." Writers are supposed to write what they know, but what could a child know about existential despair? Yet there it was, page after desperate page of it, screaming to get out of me. Like this poem that I wrote at age ten about the Black Beast—and showed to no one:

My eyes are not wet
And yet I am weeping—
I sink with the weight
Of the secret I'm keeping.
I try to run, yet cannot move
I turn to flee, yet find no door.

I close my eyes to hide the sight
And cover my ears to shut out the roar . . .
They say in the Bible, look forward to Death
Now I can laugh at the things I have read—
What fools we stupid humans are
I am dying, I am dead.

But all my poetry couldn't have been so morose, because my father thought it was wonderful. It was our closest bond. The minute Daddy got home from work, he'd toss his jacket on the kitchen chair and say, "Okay, baby, what did you write for me today?" Nothing else came first: dinner, my mother, Zach, the bills—they all had to wait until I handed over whatever I had written that day.

Even though I knew he was biased, I basked in his praise. Deep down, I suppose I realized that his attention came at the expense of the family, but I was too happy to care. He was a grown-up, after all; he knew what he was doing. And what else could we talk about at the dinner table? This wasn't meaningless triviality, like Zach's obsession with go-carts or my mother's infinite variations on who said what at work. This was Art.

Most important of all, Father Tim agreed with my father: he thought my writing was special. Father Tim was the new priest at St. Madeleine's—young and kind and so handsome he could have been a movie star. He was tall and slim and dark doe-eyed, like Gregory Peck in *Roman Holiday*. All the girls had a crush on him, including and especially me. He was my first thought in the morning, my last at night. I pictured him instead of Jesus when I prayed, which couldn't have been good. I fantasized constantly about undoing his clerical collar, but I couldn't quite figure out how I'd do it. Did it unbutton? Unsnap? Unzip? It became something of an obsession with me.

Whatever Father Tim said, I believed. He did the smartest thing any mentor could do: he set me free to read. While the other students studied geography and fractions and current events, Father Tim turned me loose on the schoolyard grounds with his personal copy of *Walden*. Lord, how I came to hate Thoreau, but I slogged through it out of my devotion to Father Tim.

Then, after his sermon one afternoon, Father Tim announced that at the end of the school year he would be moving on to a new parish in Africa. I was devastated, of course, and immediately turned to poetry to help mitigate my loss. I wanted to write him a farewell poem, something that he could keep with him always, next to his heart; something worthy of the great confidence he'd always shown in me. I remember the moment of inspiration: I was sitting in the backyard with pencil and paper, my back against my favorite elm. A leaf fluttered down at my feet—a young leaf, still green. I picked it up and played with it idly, wondering why it had met its end at such a tender age. It was still soft, still pliant: why?

A sense of urgency came over me. Every second that I sat there was a second closer to Father Tim's departure. Time pressed me like a vise, squeezing out each breath. I set the leaf down carefully and began to write what eventually turned into this:

Humpty-Dumpty's Final Stand

Passing fast to memory
Oblivion devours time
A half-fogged haze enveloping
Blank sheets of lovely empty rhyme.
In mists of better, shades of sweet
The hard and sourness compete
To edge each other off the wall:
A lost and long-lingering fall.
Thus shaded, shrouded, past repair
The aging times all muster troops—
Press closely in the gathering gray,
Rock silently on creaking stoops.

As with much of my poetry at that age, I wasn't quite sure what it meant. There was only this need, this aching need, to put my feelings into words: to constrain them, somehow, with meter and rhyme. I suppose I knew of no other way to deal with my emotions, except to distance them through metaphor.

Father Tim loved it—so much so that he typed up my childish scrawl and sent it off, along with a few of my other poems, to a professor at the nearby Claremont Colleges. A few weeks later, my father sat me down to announce the news: "Baby, you're going to college."

An associate professor of English at Pomona College, a small but highly regarded liberal arts school, thought I showed promise. Professor Tremaine was willing to take me on for several hours each week, for private counseling, to audit his classes, and to attend lectures. The rest of the time, I'd go to my regular school. But still, I was terrified. "How will I get there, and who'll take me home?" was all I could think of to say.

Since both my parents worked, transportation logistics were already a nightmare. My parents parked us at all sorts of venues—ballet and tap and baton classes for me, the Boy Scouts for Zach, and when absolutely necessary, at the O'Learys' house a few blocks away. Mrs. O'Leary always smelled like cooking sherry, and Mr. O'Leary snored on the couch for most of the day. Their son Dan, who was fifteen, wanted to be a rock star when he grew up. He had no interest whatsoever in me, except on those afternoons when everybody was elsewhere. Then he'd invite me to sit down on the couch with him, and he'd play me my favorite songs on his electric guitar, including, always, the incomparable theme from the *Hawaii Five-O* TV show.

I could have listened to that song forever. It had a simple, driving pulse that I felt down deep in my body. "Again!" I'd beg Dan, but he would never agree—not unless "I did something for him first." He'd grab my hand and take me into the bathroom and shut the door. Then he'd slide down his pants and his underwear, expose his penis and shake it at me. "Lick it," he'd order.

At ten, I knew nothing of the human anatomy. I was a shining example of the Catholic school system: devout and utterly ignorant. The first time Dan took me into the bathroom, the sight of his erect penis shocked and unnerved me. I recoiled, the warm, sour taste of nausea in my mouth. Did all men carry those things tucked inside their pants? Surely my father's didn't look like this, all red and raw and throbbing. It was ugly, and the Black Beast hated ugly things. I tried to go, but Dan had locked the door, and I had to fumble with the handle.

"If you don't do it, I'll never play *Hawaii Five-O* for you again," Dan said. He looked taller and meaner than he ever had before, and I was suddenly aware of the difference in our ages.

"Do it, or else."

I hated ultimatums. But the thought of never hearing that song again, when all I had to go through was one moment's disgust . . . Holding my nose, I leaned over and licked it. It was warm and spongy and slightly moist. Dan moaned, which frightened me.

"Are you sick?" I asked.

"No," he answered. "But you have to go now."

"What about my song?"

"Later."

"No, now." I was outraged that he was trying to slip out of our deal. Tears of anger sprang to my eyes, but I quickly blinked them away. I'd be damned if I'd let him see me cry.

Dan unlocked the door, but before he shoved me out, he put his face close to mine. I could smell the Fritos he'd eaten at lunch. "Swear," he said.

"Swear what?"

"That you were never here."

"But I was here; I'm here right now."

"Swear, or I'll tell everyone it was your idea. And I'll never play you that song again."

I swore. What else could I do? But I kept two fingers crossed behind my back. I was pretty sure what we had just done was a sin, even though I'd acted with innocent intent. Which meant I'd have to confess it someday if I wanted to safeguard my soul.

I ran out to the living room and waited at the piano stool, tapping my foot impatiently. It may seem odd that I still cared about the *Hawaii Five-O* theme after what had happened between us, but it was about far more than just the song now. Even at ten, I believed in the sanctity of contracts. I'd done what I'd done, and now it was his turn to perform.

It seemed like eons before Dan eventually came out. I moved to the other side of the room, and we carefully avoided each other's eyes. But he sat down and played *Hawaii Five-O* for me three times in a row, better than he'd ever played it before. Or maybe it just sounded better to me because now I knew its price.

My sins weighed heavily on me in those days. At ten, I guess my soul was still so relatively spotless, I felt each black mark keenly. I was obsessive about confessing every week before taking communion. It was the only thing besides poetry that made me feel clean. But tell what I'd done with Dan O'Leary to my beloved Father Tim? What would he think of me then? I have to admit, only part of me was reluctant. The Black Beast was tantalized by the thought of spilling my dirty secrets to him.

I knew the confessional was supposed to be an inviolate place, a direct line to the divine. But it was, after all, so small a space, and human beings in such close proximity can't help but turn animal, sniffing each other out. So when I stepped into the confessional the following Friday, I was acutely aware of Father Tim's presence, his warm breath through the screen, the freshly laundered scent of his vestments.

The Black Beast had been all atingle that morning. He kept urging me to dress more quickly—eat my breakfast faster—hurry, hurry to the church. It was hard to rein him in. My father noticed me wolfing down my pancakes and asked me what was the rush.

"No rush. Just hungry." Oh damn, a lie. I'd have to remember to confess that too.

I said my opening lines so fast that Father Tim had to ask me to say them again. "Once more, with feeling," he said. Talking slowly was extremely hard for the Beast when he was in this kind of mood. The pressure of unspoken thoughts and words kept building up against my tongue until I stammered. "B-bless me, Father, f-for I have sinned . . ." Finally, I spat out the canned remarks, and he asked the question I was both longing and dreading to hear: "And what are your sins?"

I was ready. "I have been impure in word and deed," I said, parroting the language I'd read so often in my catechism.

"Go on."

"Once, I lied to my father. And once, I licked a penis."

"For the lie, say ten Hail Marys," he said. "Now, what was that last part again?"

Deserved or not, priests have acquired a bad reputation for seducing children. In this case, it was the child trying to seduce the priest. Not that I wanted anything sexual from him. I only wanted to make sure that when he left, I would remain a vivid memory. I heard my voice, as if from far away. It was husky from yesterday's cheerleading practice, and I sounded far older and smokier than my ten years as I repeated, "Once, I licked a penis."

Father Tim leaned in closer to the screen. "Whose penis did you lick?"

I wasn't at all prepared for that, and my stammer came right back. "I-I'm sorry, but I can't tell you that. I swore I wouldn't."

"But God knows everything, my child."

"Then why do I have to tell you?"

He sat back, clearly stumped.

"Why did you do this thing?" he asked.

"He made me."

"You mean, he physically forced you to do it?"

"Well, no, but he gave me no other choice. And Father?"

"Yes?"

"Part of me found it quite interesting. Not the good part of me, you understand, but the part that does the nasty things, that gets me into trouble . . ." I was entering dangerous territory here, and the Black Beast abruptly stopped speaking.

"Go on."

"Well, it didn't feel at all like I'd expected. I'd thought it would be like licking an ice cream cone. But it was warm, just like a living thing. And it wasn't sweet, it was salty."

Silence from the other side of the screen, which seemed to last forever.

"Father?" I asked, and my voice was back to normal again.

I sounded just like what I was: a terrified ten-year-old girl. I wanted to ask him, "Am I damned?" but it came out "Are you mad at me?"

"No, Terri, I'm not mad at you."

I gasped. The priest is never supposed to use your name during confession. The shared pretense is that he doesn't even know who you are. You're just another repentant sinner seeking out God's grace. Father Tim had broken the sacred rules. The Black Beast was thrilled to the marrow.

"But I'm concerned," he continued. "I think you're a very special girl, and you're about to enter a brand new world. Trust me. College can be very . . ." He paused, as if searching for the right word. ". . . stimulating. Full of new ideas and new temptations. I'm worried for your soul."

"Thank you, Father," I said humbly, but the Black Beast was so excited that I had to bite down hard on my lower lip to keep from saying, "You really think I'm special?"

"If this business with the licking ever happens again, I want you to come straight to me and tell me all about it. In person," he added. "Not in confession. Here it has to remain confidential. Now promise."

"I promise," I said, knowing full well that once the Black Beast's curiosity had been aroused, my promises meant nothing. I would see Dan O'Leary again. He would play the *Hawaii Five-O* theme for me, and I would lick his penis. Father Tim lived in a make-believe world, all flickering candles and incense. I lived in the real, transactional world, where beasts were bigger than all the best intentions. I sighed.

"I'm really sorry," I said.

"I know. Now say your Act of Contrition. Slowly, like you mean it."

"Oh my God, I am heartily sorry for having offended Thee, and I detest all my sins, because I dread the loss of Heaven and the pains of Hell; but most of all, because I love Thee, my God, who art all good and deserving of all my love . . ."

I spoke as slowly as I could, putting my whole heart into my words. But I was speaking all the while to Father Tim, not to God. Desire, as would always be the case with me, had the final say.

My father found a student who could drive me to the college and pick me up. As the time grew close for me to start, I became increasingly nervous. So the Sunday before my first class, my whole family trooped to the campus for a tour, to familiarize me with my new environment.

Pomona College was like a jewel in a garden, many of the buildings magnificently weathered and covered with ivy, the landscaping lush. This was no mere community college, I realized. It was the real deal. I felt overwhelmed by the tour. How would I find the bathrooms? What if I got lost? How could I locate a pay phone, in case of some dire emergency?

I'd assumed that the family would all go out to dinner together afterward, to celebrate my new adventure. But my father headed straight for home, and once we got there, my mother made a beeline for her bedroom. Danielle, the latest in a long string of babysitters, was waiting for us at the front door.

"What do you think?" she asked Zach and me. "Plain or pepperoni?"

"Kung pao shrimp!" Zach shouted.

I shot my father a look. He shrugged and glanced away. "Your mother wants to go out to dinner."

"Fine, then let's go out."

"Just the two of us, sweetie."

I felt a pang, like I'd been smacked by a dodgeball. "Why?"

Another shrug.

"If I get her to change her mind, can I go?" I asked.

He bent down and whispered, "Tell her you're really nervous about tomorrow."

I skittered down the hall and knocked on my mother's door.

"Go away," she said. "I'm dressing."

"I know," I said. "I want to watch."

To my surprise, she let me in. "You can untangle those," she said, pointing to the long string of pearls my father had given her for their anniversary. "But be careful about it, and don't touch anything else."

I was dismayed when I saw the spread on the bed: the beaded clutch, the sheer black stockings, the blue silk dress with the portrait neckline that was my father's favorite. And worst of all, the mink stole. I felt helpless against that mink stole. My mother was unassailable in it: beautiful, elegant, confident. But most of all, she was a woman, and I was still a girl.

I bent over her pearls and said, "You know, Mom, I'm really, really nervous about tomorrow."

She didn't look up from fastening her garters. "You'll be fine; you always are."

"It would really help me if I could go out with you and Daddy tonight, just to talk things over."

"You can talk things over with Zach."

I snorted. "All Zach wants to talk about are go-carts and *Star Trek*. Come on, pretty please? It's my first day at college, and I want to do it right."

She finally looked at me. "Tonight is for your father and me. You are not, I repeat, *not* coming along."

I couldn't remember the last time my parents had gone out together as a couple. Sometime last year, maybe. I'd almost foiled that time too by running a fever. But at the last minute, my mother had caught me holding the thermometer up to the lamp.

"But Mom," I whined. She stopped me before I could say another word. Grabbing my arm, she turned me to face her.

"I said no. Tonight is my night, and you're staying home."

The Black Beast didn't like to be touched, and he especially didn't like that word *no*. A flush of anger surged through my blood.

"You don't love me!" I shouted. "You never did!"

"Not when you're being a spoiled brat."

I had to get out of that room, away from those pearls, which were just begging to be ripped apart and flung into every corner. But even at the outer limits of my control, I knew that I couldn't let my father see me like this. As far as he was concerned, I was a sweet and even-tempered child, intense and serious for my age, but obedient nonetheless. I didn't want him to meet the Black Beast face to face.

I ran down the hallway to my room and started wildly rearranging things. Sometimes that distracted the Beast: overturning the furniture, ripping down all my books, then putting them back alphabetically. That night, however, it didn't help. The Black Beast seethed. The pressure inside my head felt like it would explode. I had to do something, quick—so I grabbed my old cheerleading baton and did a couple of spins in front of my mirrored closet door.

"We're leaving now!" my father yelled from the kitchen. I heard the front door close.

I spun myself around again. This time I couldn't stand what I saw: a little girl, ugly and scrawny, unworthy of love. I kept on spinning. All I could hear was my mother saying "No" to me. Louder, with each spin:

"No."

"No!"

"NO!"

"Kill it," the Black Beast whispered.

I swung the baton back as far as my arms could reach, then smashed it into the full-length mirror. My face shattered into a gazillion pieces, glass shards flying around the room. I stepped back, a little stunned but satisfied. The room was silent. I'd murdered my mother's voice.

The next morning, we were in such a tizzy getting me off to college that I somehow managed to get away with my rather lame explanation about the broken mirror. I said that I was practicing my twirls, and the baton flew out of my hands. My mother sized me up but said nothing. Their big evening out had apparently been a success: my father actually pecked her on the cheek as she was leaving for work. Then he dropped me off at the Pomona College gate, at the northern boundary of the campus. The gate was inscribed, "Let only the eager, thoughtful, and reverent enter here."

It scared the hell out of me.

It was 1970, the height of hippiedom and the free love/flower child movement. I stood at the massive, ivy-covered gate in my Catholic schoolgirl uniform: blue-and-gray plaid pleated skirt, crisp Peter Pan–collared shirt, kneesocks, and shiny black spit-polished shoes. Everywhere I looked was anarchy: students smoking, kissing, arguing. One couple was lying on the grass, their groins locked together like magnets. To me, people seemed not so much dressed as strategically undressed, consciously di-sheveled. Hair was long and prominent—tousled, unkempt—on the boys as well as the girls.

I reached back and touched my own long and cautious braid that my mother had fixed for me that morning. I tugged at the rubber band holding it in place and shook my head until my face was enveloped in a reddish-blonde cloud. "Cool," said a passing woman in tattered bell-bottom jeans. That was all the encouragement I needed. With some bravado restored, I went to find Professor Tremaine.

I remembered enough from yesterday's tour to make my way to his office. It was on the top floor of a small brick building across from a big, thriving oak. My legs itched at the sight of that tree: it was prime for climbing, the branches sturdy and not too far apart, the bark just rough enough to get a purchase. I eyed it like a professional, which is what I was rapidly becoming. Over the past few months, I'd climbed every tree in my own backyard at least a dozen times, and there wasn't a sign pole in the whole neighborhood that I hadn't made my Everest.

Climbing had quickly become second only to poetry in my pantheon, an amazing fact considering that I hadn't a tomboy bone in my body. My mother dressed me like a delicate thing—all white cotton eyelet and lace filigree—and expected me to return home just as pristine. She wouldn't even allow me to go barefoot in summer, for fear I'd pick up a dreaded "something" from lawns less well-manicured than our own.

It made for a difficult coexistence with the neighborhood toughs. One afternoon a few months back, Doug Dyson had called me a chickenshit and given me an Indian burn because I refused to climb the sign pole at the end of our street. I was wearing a dress; my mother would kill me; plus I didn't know how to do it. These seemed like three very good reasons to me for refusing, but I didn't dare share them with Doug. I just shook my head and glared at him mutely, like the village idiot.

That night, though, after the street lights came on and all the kids had gone home, I snuck out of the house and climbed that damned pole. Not right away, of course. I felt heavy and clumsy and couldn't figure out where to put my hands and feet. Gradually, I discovered that if I pressed my hips really hard against the metal, it anchored me and freed up the rest of my body to move. Ever so slowly, inch by inch, I dragged myself up.

Three-quarters of the way there, I noticed a flurry of sensations in my pelvic region, but I ignored them. Ever since I'd begun playing the *Hawaii Five-O* game with Dan O'Leary, I'd become aware of strange and sudden stirrings "down there," a place that had always been dormant.

But by the time I reached the top of the pole, I couldn't ignore what was going on between my legs. I was pounding and pulsing and throbbing, caught up in a mighty current. It was as if I were being thrust to the edge of a great waterfall: waiting, resisting, until finally . . . release. Then falling, falling, falling forever.

I held on to the sign pole for dear life, not sure when these incredible sensations in my body would end, and even less sure I ever wanted them to. I had a nagging sense that whatever this was, it felt too good to be good for me. It was on a par with rubbing up naked against my mother's mink stole, or running barefoot in summer: too wickedly delicious to be allowed.

When my heart finally slowed to its normal rhythm, I slid down the pole—only to be assaulted by a dizzying rush of anxiety once my feet touched the pavement. I'd always known that my mind was capable of astonishing intensity. Now I knew that my body was too. I didn't know how to feel about this discovery: exhilarated, proud, or terrified? Was I a freak or a prodigy? I saw no middle ground. I clung to the pole, trying to will myself into tranquility, which never works no matter how hard you try.

I didn't know back then that heightened sexuality is a common feature of childhood bipolar disorder. As it was, I was left feeling lost and bewildered, certain of only one thing:

whatever had just happened to me, I absolutely had to keep it a secret. Yet another secret. I wondered if by the time I became an adult, there would be any room left in my storehouse of secrets, or would I someday be crushed under the sheer weight of them?

So I told no one about my experience, but you can bet I took to climbing trees and poles with a vengeance after that. "The Feeling," as I called it, didn't happen every time, but the intermittent reinforcement made me crave it all the more. As I stood before the campus oak, I felt a familiar flash of desire. That's what I needed: a quick hit of the Feeling. Then I'd have confidence enough for anything.

I looked at my watch. I had a few minutes left before my appointment with Professor Tremaine. But my uniform was neatly pressed, and my shoes were freshly shined, and—"Oh, shut up and do it," the Black Beast snarled. I glanced around. No one seemed to be watching me, so I shrugged off my backpack and shimmied up the tree. It was, as I'd suspected, an easy climb, the trunk firm and rigid between my thighs. I scurried up until I was safely nestled among the thickly woven branches. Then I slowed down—way, way down—and rocked my hips from side to side and round and round until I found the perfect rhythm. I closed my eyes and thought of Father Tim and the elusive catch on that clerical collar. I wondered if his skin underneath would be pale and soft, or taut and tanned as the rest of him . . .

It didn't take much, just the thought of pressing my lips to his bare neck, before the Feeling flooded me—wave after wave of it, lifting me high above the tree, weightless as a wisp of cloud. But then the Black Beast made some kind of animal sounds, which quickly brought me down to earth and back into my body. In my wild rush to get up the tree and find the Feeling, I hadn't noticed that there was an open window not far away, almost within reach. I couldn't see inside from my angle, but I broke out in a sweat nonetheless, afraid that I'd been seen or heard doing whatever it was I did to the tree.

"See what you made me do?" I snapped, but the Black Beast felt smug and satisfied.

"Now you're ready for poetry," he said.

I was, but I was ten minutes late. I slid down the tree, grabbed my backpack, and bounded up the narrow stairs, taking two steps at a time. Professor Tremaine's was the very first office at the top. He was on the phone and waved me to a seat. I looked around me, breathless.

It was chaos; books and papers stacked everywhere, which deeply disturbed the neat freak inside me. But the most prominent sight of all was the painting hanging above his desk: an enormous cracked egg, out of which spilled dozens, maybe hundreds, of little green peas.

Why peas? Was it some kind of veiled sexual reference that I didn't get? Ever since meeting Dan O'Leary's penis, I'd felt like the whole world was one big erotic in-joke, and I was missing the punch line. I heard and saw sex in everything—and the last thing I wanted was to seem unhip or naïve or, worse yet, innocent. I was, after all, in college now, even if I still went to fourth grade on the side.

Nervously, I took a dozen or so books from the nearest untidy pile and rearranged them neatly on the desk. Unfortunately, one of the books was *Walden*, which naturally made me shudder.

"Are you cold?" asked a voice. I looked up and saw Professor Tremaine leaning back in his chair, studying me. "I could close the window."

With his young, bearded, slightly sad face and brilliant blue eyes, he was the spitting image of the Jesus Christ in my Sunday psalm book. I instantly felt overawed and couldn't think of a thing to say. The Black Beast felt no such qualms. The first words out of my mouth were, "I like your dirty painting. I'm surprised they let you hang it there."

He blinked several times, like a startled owl. "Dirty? Really?" He looked more closely at me, then at the painting, then at me, then ran his fingers through his beard. "One of my students painted it. To be honest, I'm not sure what it means. What makes you think it's dirty?"

"Well, the egg is so smooth and white and looks so pure, but then you crack it open and there are all these nasty little peas inside, like dirty thoughts that just can't wait to get out." I blushed furiously, in spite of my desperate desire to seem cool.

"What's the title, anyway?" I asked.

"*Egg with Peas*," he said.

"Oh." Deflated, I dropped my eyes. They rested on *Walden*, and again I shuddered. Professor Tremaine raised an eyebrow.

"It's just—that book," I said.

"You've read it?"

"I tried. I don't get it."

"What don't you get?"

"I don't know." I squirmed in my seat and pulled up one of my kneesocks. "It's boring."

"You think so? That's a shame. To me, it's pure poetry."

I kicked the rung of my chair. I was embarrassed, and when I'm embarrassed, I pretend to be annoyed. "Poetry? Hah! It doesn't even rhyme."

An eager light flickered behind his eyes, like a hunter who's spotted fresh meat. "Since when does poetry have to rhyme?"

"Since Shakespeare. And Dr. Seuss." Both seemed like equally weighty precedent to me.

"Shakespeare doesn't always rhyme, you know. At least, not in the way you're thinking. Not like your poetry." He picked up a volume from the windowsill. "Here, I'll read you the soliloquy from *Hamlet*, and you tell me what you think."

I understood very little of what he read, but still, I was moved. If only I had been able to write such beautiful words when I was seven, I probably never would have taken my mother's pills. Why die, when you can write? Professor Tremaine finished reading, and I sighed.

"Wonderful, isn't it?" he asked.

I nodded.

"Does it rhyme?"

"No."

"Is it poetry?"

"Yes."

"Then that's going to be our mission. To set you free from rhyme."

I suddenly felt trapped. Lose my beloved rhymes? They were the only things in the world that brought some order and symmetry to my life. I never knew when my father was going to slam that front door for good, or which fight was going to be their last. I never knew when the Black Beast was going to take control. Would I be sunny and cheery and talk too much and spin a little too fast that day? Or would I feel crushed to the ground, too heavy to move, unable to summon the semblance of a smile? All I could really count on for sure was that Zach was going to be in his room.

Besides, my father loved rhyme.

Professor Tremaine continued: ". . . and on Friday, I'm going to have you come to the Visiting Scholars lecture. This week it's Galway Kinnell, the poet. He's very famous and very good." He smiled. "And his poetry doesn't rhyme."

The egg in the painting looked down on me, the crack in its shell now resembling a malevolent grin.

The professor stood up. "I think that's enough for today," he said. "Except for one thing." He reached over and, before I could pull back, plucked a leaf out of my hair and handed it to me. Then I think he winked, but I wasn't sure, and I wasn't about to stay and find out. I practically ran out of his office.

I passed the oak without a second thought and headed back toward the college gate. A woman was leaning up against the ivy, obscuring the words "thoughtful and reverent." She was kissing a man who had his hand down her shirt, which gave me a glimpse of her writhing bare breast.

More sex. Less rhyme. That seemed the direction my world was headed, and I can't say I was pleased.

I tried writing a poem that afternoon when I got back from the college, but without the mesmerizing magic of rhyme, the words just seemed like random letters sprawled across the page. And what was there to say, anyhow? Probably everyone who'd ever written a decent poem had enjoyed some kind of sex, and that's what they were writing about, either directly or in between the lines. It wasn't fair. It was discrimination against good Catholic girls.

It was clearly time to climb a tree.

I chose my most reliable: the big old elm behind my bedroom window. It was the quickest and easiest conduit to the Feeling—usually. But that afternoon, I climbed and climbed until my thighs were too sore to grip the branches. The foulness of my temper increased with every unsuccessful, unsatisfying inch. By then, I'd climbed so high that I wasn't sure how I would get back down. I settled into a nook between two big branches and pulled out my pencil and a scrap of paper from my back pocket.

I was dizzy, not just from my precarious perch but from the lack of rhyme to anchor me. I tried to picture Father Tim's face, but what was the point? The Feeling was gone, Father Tim was as good as gone, and there was nothing left for me but the empty page, stripped of all its comfort.

I felt so lonely my ribs ached. But I struggled on and eventually wrote this:

Desolataire

What pain to live on when one dies
What shame to keep the whole thing going
Only because one doesn't know—is
Scared of—what might be beyond.
What harm could be in going forward
What keeps one here so long a time
After the fire and fun and fancy
After the lights go down for good?
What dark dark days stretch out before me
What is there here to keep me still
If but I knew I would have stilled it
How long ago would have been gone.
Whatever—once again I sigh
Whatever—shrug and turn away
To yet more sorrow, desolation
Empty yawn of time. What life.

I'd just finished fiddling with the last line when I heard my
mother's voice from very far away: "Zach! Terri Lynn! Time for
dinner!" Enough with feeding my soul; I was famished. But it
was a long way back to earth. When I finally managed to scramble down, my legs were all aquiver, and my palms were studded
with splinters.

I washed up as quickly as I could, yanking out the larg-
est splinters, driving the smaller ones deeper in with my im-
patience. "Out, damn you!" I snarled, not even caring that

swearing was a sin I'd someday have to confess. The pain didn't bother me—in fact, it was a welcome distraction from the nastiness of my mood. Free verse obviously didn't agree with me. I felt feral; I felt savage. The Black Beast was just itching to get out, hyperalert to any pretext for provocation.

While my mother was cleaning up after dinner, she explained to Zach and me that she was going to have to go out for an hour or so; some kind of meeting at the school. Zach's grades, never good, had been slipping, and his teacher was worried. "Your father's going to be late, so that means Zach will be in charge," she told us. "I expect to come home and find the dishes washed, your homework done, and the two of you in your beds. Is that understood?"

I looked over at Zach, disgusted. His chest was puffed out like a blowfish. He'd been campaigning for this for months. "I'm thirteen and three-quarters," he wheedled, over and over again. "I don't need no stinkin' babysitter."

"No, what you need is to study your grammar," my father replied.

"It's a joke, Dad," Zach said, rolling his eyes.

My father eventually relented, on one condition: "But you'll have to promise to watch over your sister."

Zach held up his Boy Scout ring and promised.

After my mother left, Zach did boss me around a bit, making sure I washed and dried all the dishes and took out the evening's trash (which was normally his chore). In spite of my disgruntled mood, I let him do it, a little impressed by his new superiority—but mostly because I assumed that afterward we'd get to do something fun. We didn't spend much time together outside of school, what with all my studying and his—well, go-carts and whatever else it was he did in his room.

But after the kitchen was spic-and-span, Zach grabbed a stack of manuals that had come in the mail that afternoon, and disappeared. "Go do your homework," he told me over his shoulder. I sat down to my geometry lesson and studied for exactly five seconds. No, it wasn't possible. The Black Beast wanted to play.

I picked up the phone. Although I wasn't allowed to make phone calls without permission, it felt soothing somehow to break a rule. The only problem was, I didn't know who to call. It was weird. Technically, I was popular: a cheerleader, class officer, all of that. But I didn't really have many close friends that I could just call up to chat. They all lived too far away: St. Madeleine's was in another area code, and my mother watched our pennies. There was always my neighbor Katie, though. Despite the fact that she was a year younger than I was and went to (Heaven forbid) public school, she lived just down the street. I called her up.

"Hello?"

The minute I heard her voice, I launched into my tale of woe: my mother said this, my brother did that, the professor wouldn't let me use rhyme—

Katie interrupted. "Terri, you're doing it again."

"What?"

"Talking so fast I can't understand you."

"Okay." I took a breath and tried to slow down. "Wanna go climb poles?"

"I can't. The streetlights are on."

"So?"

"I'm not allowed to go out after the streetlights go on. And neither are you," she added.

"Mama's girl." I hung up without saying good-bye and ran down the hall to Zach's room. I kicked on his door. "Zach! Wanna go climb poles?"

"I told you to go do your homework," he said through the door.

"I don't want to."

"Do it."

"No."

"I'm in charge now."

I kicked his door again, so hard it left a mark. "You're supposed to be taking care of me," I said, but so softly he couldn't hear it.

"Please?" I shouted. I hated being nice to him, but my agitation was getting mixed in with loneliness now, and loneliness always made me polite.

When I got no response, I went back to the kitchen, looked at my lopsided diagram of a hexagon, and ripped it into pieces. If the Black Beast wanted to play, so be it. I wasn't supposed to touch Zach's bike—the brand new ten-speed he'd gotten for Christmas—but I went in the garage and unlocked it. (Unbeknownst to Zach, I knew his combination. It was always the same: 0-0-7. Zach had ambitions.) It was harder to ride than my own old-fashioned bike, which had big wheels and a beribboned basket. But once I managed to mount it and get a rhythm going, it went like the wind.

I headed straight for the park, a few blocks away—the one I was never allowed to go to by myself because "there might be strangers there." Strangers were bad, of course. I didn't quite know why, but then, I'd never met one.

It was a beautiful night, just chilly enough so that I appreciated my sweater. The moon was almost full, so there was plenty of light to steer by, although a coal-black cat nearly crossed my path, and I had a nasty swerve trying to avoid it. All around me, people were snug and safe in their neat little homes, in their neat little lives, watching TV and mindlessly munching. I alone knew what freedom tasted like: strong and sweet and just slightly bitter, like my father's morning coffee. I felt immensely grown-up, zooming down Benson Avenue, using my arms to signal left and right turns even though there were no cars to see me do it.

But once I really got going, I abandoned all pretense of caution. I indulged my craving for speed, more speed, pumping my knees so fast and hard they felt like automatic pistons. The wind kicked up then, burning my cheeks and making tears stream out of the corners of my eyes. They stung, but freedom has its cost, and I never felt so wide awake in my life.

I knew what I wanted: the swings. For whatever reason, vigorous swinging always made me feel terrific. My own ups and downs disappeared when I swooshed up and swooshed back, letting gravity be my master. We used to have a swing set in our own backyard when I was very little, but my mother thought I used it too recklessly—I always insisted on sailing too high.

The swings at the park were deserted. In fact, the whole park was deserted, except for a man standing by a tree near the rec center, with his back to me. A stranger. I shivered, but the Black Beast didn't care. Plus I was going too fast to slow down. I glided up noiselessly behind him. He was doing something to his pants. I heard a zip, then he whipped out his penis and peed on the tree.

I screeched to a halt. He turned around and hastily fumbled to zip up his pants.

"Sorry about that," he said. There was a black hole where his front tooth should have been.

I ought to have been terrified, but the Black Beast knew no fear. Still half drunk from the exhilaration of my ride, I waived my hand airily in the direction of his penis. "No big deal," I said. "I've seen plenty of those."

He moved a few steps closer. "My name's Tom," he said. "What are you doing out here, all by yourself?"

For some reason, maybe because he was a stranger and I knew I'd never see him again, the usual rule of secrecy didn't apply. I felt compelled to tell him the truth. "The Black Beast wanted to play, and nobody would play with me."

"Who's the Black Beast?"

"Um, he's—it's—just somebody I know." I decided to switch gears. "Wanna go climb poles?"

He put a hand on my front tire, then moved it up to caress the handlebar. "That's a mighty nice bike you've got there," he said. He was close enough now that I could smell him, and the smell was overpowering—not quite wine, not quite pee, but an overwhelming combination of the two. The Black Beast didn't like funny smells.

"I just forgot. I've got to draw a hexagon." I backed away. He followed me.

"Don't go so soon. We were just getting acquainted." He smiled, and the moon beamed into the gap in his teeth. I was suddenly frightened. I jerked the handlebar out of his grasp, jumped on the pedals, and didn't look back.

"Tell the Black Beast I said hello!" Tom yelled after me, but as I sped away, I realized that the Black Beast was nowhere to be found. He and all his reckless bravado had deserted me too.

When I got home, my mother was frantic. She grabbed me and held me close to her chest. Then she shook me, hard, by the shoulders.

"Where have you been? We've been worried sick about you." Zach stood behind her, white-faced. "I called all the neighbors. Katie said you'd gone somewhere to climb poles. Your father's out looking for you now."

I heard the key turn in the lock. My father came in. I rushed to him and started crying. I was genuinely upset and scared, but I also knew that tears usually headed off his anger. It was a desperate moment that called for desperate measures.

"Zach told me I could go out," I lied.

"What the hell?" My father glared at Zach. "We trusted you." Zach exploded. "It's a total lie! I never told her anything!"

"Then how did I get the combination to his bike?" In spite of my tears, I played my trump card smoothly.

"Well?" my father asked Zach.

"She's lying. You know she's lying. And you always take her side." I couldn't believe it. Zach was crying. Zach never cried.

He'd get red in the face, like Daddy, but the tears would never come. Now they were pouring down his face, mingling with the snot from his nose.

My mother pulled a Kleenex out of her purse and gently wiped his face. I watched her tender gesture with a mixture of resentment and relief. I felt sorry for Zach, but not sorry enough to take back my lie.

"Jack," my mother said, softly. "I think you and I should talk about this."

"There's nothing to talk about," my father said. "I told you we couldn't trust him. He's too irresponsible. Anything could have happened to her."

I'll never forget the look on Zach's face. It was like stabbing him with the fork all over again, but worse.

He was grounded, of course. As was I. "You should have known better," my father said.

The problem was, I did.

In spite of being grounded, I was allowed to attend the Galway Kinnell reading later that week. I was impressed by the turnout: it was late afternoon, but the auditorium was packed, not just with students but with faculty and other adults from the community. Professor Tremaine found me a seat right in front and showed me where he'd be sitting, a few rows behind.

My mood had greatly improved by then, so much so that I was tapping my toes and twisting all the way round in my seat to see who was coming in next. Although I'd been scared about going to the reading alone, now I was relieved. My mother would surely have admonished me to sit still, and no way, Jose! I just couldn't. I was too excited, but it was more than that. Ever since that scary night in the park, my thoughts had been steadily picking up speed, to the point where they now raced around in my head like bumper cars run amok. Which made me think of go-carts, which made me think of Zach, which was not good. I was truly sorry for what I had done to him, but he still refused to speak to me.

To try to keep my mind from thoughts of Zach, I stared at the young man next to me: a student, no doubt, from his scruffy beard and lived-in jeans and—oh my God!—bare feet. How had he gotten in here without any shoes? I looked around in indignation, but there was no one to complain to, except perhaps Professor Tremaine. But something told me that a man who preferred his poetry stripped of rhyme wouldn't care about naked feet. He'd probably like them better that way.

The word *naked* sent a chill down my spine, and try as I might, I couldn't resist staring down at those feet. They were uncommonly large and ugly, with smidgens of dirt in between the toes. I longed to wipe them clean with my hair, like Mary Magdalene did to Jesus. (But Jesus at least had worn sandals.)

"Jesus," of course, made me think of sin, and sin made me think about Zach again, so the bumper cars were right back where they'd started. I put my head down in between my hands and groaned. "Are you okay?" asked the man with the dirty toes. But the lights were flooding the stage by then and I was already well onto the next thought. "Shhhh," I said rudely. "It's starting."

Maybe it was the lighting. Maybe it was my close proximity

to the stage or the heat from the densely packed bodies. But when Galway Kinnell stood at the podium and the applause swelled up all around me, I felt dizzy, overcome. I wish I could remember the timbre of his voice or exactly what he looked like. All I recall is a shock of dark hair hanging over one eye and a rakish grin. But I knew then that he was the handsomest man I'd ever seen—handsomer even than Father Tim—and his words were like butterflies, darting around me, fluttering in the light.

They were sexual. Deeply sexual. At first that made me fidget and squirm, and once I even accidentally touched my seatmate's dirty toes with my foot. I was afraid that someone who knew me—a neighbor, a nun, one of my classmates' parents—might somehow find me sitting here, listening to these dangerously dirty words. But gradually, when no one came to yank me out of my seat, I leaned back and surrendered. I knew it was wrong, terribly wrong, to be listening, but I did. The butterflies flew into my open mouth, and I swallowed quite a few.

The passage that struck me the hardest was perhaps among Kinnell's simplest: he was merely describing two mosquitoes making love on top of the poem he was writing. But it floored me. To think of a world where even the tiniest things—mosquitoes, for God's sake—were at it all around you! I realized then that the reason I had been feeling so out of sorts was because I was trying to deny the elemental nature of the universe. Sex was everywhere, it was all around me, there was simply no escaping it.

A dread began to fill my heart; a guilt like none I'd ever known. All those secret afternoons with Dan O'Leary. The trees, so many of them, that I'd climbed in pursuit of the elusive

Feeling. I knew exactly what the Feeling was now, because I felt something akin to it listening to Galway Kinnell read his poems. The Feeling was sex.

All this time I'd been having sex, and I didn't even know it. And as the Catholic night follows the Catholic day, that could mean only one thing: I must be pregnant.

I rubbed my hand against my belly. It felt a little swollen to me, although last night had been spaghetti and meatballs night, and my mother's meatballs never quite agreed with me. Still, there was enough of a protrusion there to cause me real concern.

I had to get home. I craned my neck to see Professor Tremaine, but I couldn't quite catch sight of him. I couldn't just get up and leave—I was in the very first row, and everybody would see. Maybe they'd even see that I was pregnant, and rumors would start flying, and I'd be banished from Pomona College forever. I stared up at the podium, willing Galway Kinnell to finish his everlasting words, but he just kept speaking as if nothing whatsoever were wrong.

More sex, less rhyme, infiltrating my pores. I stopped up my ears, but I could still hear him talking.

Humming furiously to myself, I tried to remember what my mother had said about how a girl gets pregnant. She'd sat me down one afternoon a year or so back with one of her medical textbooks and shown me pictures of things with odd names like labia and uterus and hymen. It wasn't the kind of book that I liked—there were no horses or heroines or derring-do, just rows and rows of dull, dry text and tiny illustrations. I understood that a baby might emerge from all these complicated words, but the

THE DARK SIDE OF INNOCENCE | 89

how and the why of it slipped right by me. Now I wished I'd listened harder.

Getting pregnant was probably the worst thing that could happen to a girl. It was surely the end of the world for me. The Black Beast stepped up like an orchestra conductor and, with a single tap of his baton, changed the tempo in my brain. I could feel my mood begin to plummet. I stared at my seatmate's hairy, dirty toes and longed to bury my face in their warmth. They too, like me, were nasty.

And then at last came the sound I'd been aching to hear: applause. Not end-of-the-poem but end-of-the-evening applause. I hoped that I could make a quick getaway, find my ride, and make it home to bed as soon as humanly possible. Not that that would make me any less pregnant, but everything just seemed better somehow from underneath my blue flannel sheets.

But Professor Tremaine had other plans. Even before the applause had died down, he'd grabbed me by the hand. "Come on, you've got to meet him," he said, and he led me down the aisle to the stage, where a line was already forming. He stepped in front, and pulled me up beside him. "This is the girl I was telling you about," he said to Galway Kinnell.

Kinnell stopped signing books for a moment, looked me up and down, and said something witty. I know it was witty because everyone laughed, but for the life of me, I can't remember what he said because I wasn't paying attention. I was too busy holding my stomach in; too busy noticing the ice floe creeping up my back, inching along my neck and shoulders, solidifying in a frozen attempt at a smile.

"She's a shy one," said Kinnell, and he grabbed a book off the pile at his elbow and scribbled in it, "For Terri, writing poems." Then he drew a little stick figure in a chair, hunched over a table, holding a pen. Years later, I would cherish that silly drawing and brief inscription. At that moment, however, all I could think was, I'm pregnant and there will be no more poems for me, ever. With rhyme or without.

Kinnell held out the book to me. It was so hard to get my body to move, like unsticking burnt fudge from the bottom of a pan, but I forced my hand to reach out and take it. "Thank you," I mumbled. To my surprise, Kinnell put his own hand on top of mine. For a moment, the briefest of eternities, I could feel the shape of his fingers, the texture of his skin, the warmth of his touch. And that's when I knew I was truly doomed: I liked it.

By the time I got home, I was exhausted. I tried to go straight to my bedroom, but my parents were waiting up for me. I could tell they'd been arguing—over what, I didn't know. Money, no doubt, or the mysterious Rebecca. My mother's cheeks were flushed, my father's lips were stern and pursed. But he broke into an eager smile when I walked into the kitchen. "So, how was it?" he asked. "Tell me everything."

"It was very"—I cast about for the nearest evasive word—"educational."

"Did you like it?"

I searched his eyes for a clue. Could he be trusted with the truth? I found my answer in their shining depths. No, he was too proud of me. I couldn't risk ruining his dream of the perfect little girl. So I gave him the closest I could come to truth.

"To be honest," I said, "I was scared."

"Ah." He sat back in his chair with a satisfied sigh. "Now *that's* good poetry."

I glanced over at my mother. She was staring at the tile floor. Her arms were crossed, and her cheeks were still a ruddy red, as if the blood beneath them was bursting to escape. I knew just how it felt.

"You know, I'm really tired," I said. "Can we talk about this tomorrow?"

"At least tell me how many people were there," my father said. "And what did Professor Tremaine have to say?"

My mother glanced up. "Jack," she snapped. "Let her go to bed."

I leaned over and kissed my father good night. "Do you want a cup of cocoa?" he asked. I realized then that he didn't want me to leave, but it was too late. I couldn't protect him.

"Bed," my mother insisted, and she kissed me firmly on the cheek and gave me a little push from behind. I wasn't ten steps away when I heard their argument resume. Sure enough, Rebecca. I didn't stop to listen.

When I reached my room, I quickly slipped off all my clothes. My fingers were trembling, and it was hard to undo the buttons on my cardigan. I didn't want to move, I wanted just to stand there in unconfirmed ignorance forever. But I knew I couldn't. The pregnancy would announce itself whether I wanted it to or not. I had to know for sure.

I finally managed to slip free of my sweater. I kicked my clothes to one side and stepped into the tiny bathroom that adjoined my room. There was a full-length mirror in there, leaning against the wall. Glancing reluctantly at my naked body, I noticed that my arms and thighs were covered in goose pimples. I was so slender, my breasts barely buds. My stomach looked disproportionately large in contrast, but I knew that fear was affecting my perspective. Steeling myself, I sat down on the floor, facing the mirror. I started to spread my legs—but I wasn't ready yet. I knelt and made the sign of the Cross.

"Dear God," I prayed, "please let there be nothing." I said the same exact prayer to Mary Magdalene. I figured she, of all people, could understand sin. And then I spread my legs.

I wasn't quite sure what I expected to see, having never really examined this part of my body before (and certainly not from this angle). It looked just like a sideways mouth, with one lip slightly bigger than the other. The lips were a pretty, rosy pink, as if someone had tinted them with lipstick. Gingerly, I reached down and touched myself. When it didn't hurt, I grew bolder. I parted the lips and exposed the unknown inner sanctum between them. This was where babies came from, I was pretty sure I remembered from my mother's lecture. I closed my eyes tight and asked Mary Magdalene to come hold my hand. Then I opened them and peered into the mirror.

What I saw was tiny—smaller than my thumbnail, but ever so unmistakably there. A baby. A fetus, really, all curled up inside itself. It looked remarkably like a little pink sea horse.

The room got unbearably bright, and the walls started

whirling. My grasp on reality was so slippery by then, I felt like I was sliding in and out of consciousness. I pressed my palms against the cold tile floor to steady me. Sometimes when the Black Beast got really excited, clouds looked like faces and faces looked like clouds and chairs started dancing behind my back, but I was usually able to close my eyes and make those things go away. I knew that my mind was all in a tumble, but was it possible I was seeing things that weren't really there? Only crazy people did that. Zach always said I was crazy. Was he right?

Was he, wasn't he, was he, wasn't he, and all the while the walls kept on whirling until I couldn't stand it another minute. I snapped my legs together, then forced myself to look again. There it was, the sea horse baby: irrefutable proof that I was pregnant. I began to shake. Where could life possibly go from here?

I thought back to when I was seven years old, to my amateur-ish attempt at suicide with my mother's pills. Now that I was ten, surely I could devise a more effective strategy. I knew where my father kept his straight-edge razors; and my mother was taking many more pills than she used to. It wouldn't be easy to get my hands on them, but I could manage somehow. I was so much older and wiser now . . .

Yes, suicide was clearly the answer, with one major flaw. Up until now, ten had been an exhilarating year, chock full of adventures and discoveries. Who knew what further pleasures an elm could yield? I wanted to know everything. I wanted to stand at the college gate and watch the students kissing and fondling each other, their long hair loose and unruly in the wind. I wanted to catch a couple of mosquitoes going at it, swooning in ecstasy. I wanted to rid my world of rhyme.

I didn't want to die.

There was only one alternative to suicide that I could think of, and it was far more intimidating than mere death: I could tell my mother. She was, after all, a registered nurse, but more than that, she was used to dealing with difficult things. She was the one who paid the bills, who made sure that we were clothed and fed. My father was very good with hopes and dreams, but he didn't like to be bothered with problems. "Go ask your mother" was the litany of my childhood. Daddy was the bright star in our firmament, and I used to think my mother was the gravity, always pulling him down. But now I suspected that gravity might just be necessary to keep a star up in the sky.

I suddenly longed to hear her voice; even raised in anger, my mother had a lovely voice. I wanted to feel her arms around me, her smooth, cool cheek pressed close to mine. I wanted to hear her say, "Hush now, darling, it will be all right." She'd never said those words to me before—my mother was not a "hush, now" sort of woman. But perhaps the extremity of my circumstances would soften her. Perhaps it would even bring us closer. We would fight this thing together, and we would beat it.

I could hear the Black Beast snickering, but I ignored him. Without my consciously willing it to, a cry escaped me: "Mom!" Then louder: "Mom!" Then full lung power: "*MOM!*"

I scampered into bed and pulled the covers up to my chin. I wasn't ready for her to see the sea horse baby yet; it would take a powerful bit of explaining. My bedside clock kept ticking,

ticking, and still she didn't come. I yelled again, so loud it hurt my throat: "*MOM!*" This time I got back a muffled reply from the direction of the kitchen: "What is it? I'm busy."

"I need you!" What more could I say?

Clocks must have a bit of the Black Beast in them too. One minute they seem to go so fast, the next they're barely moving. I watched the second hand sweep the dial: time was passing, precious seconds as the baby was growing inside me. We had to stop him, stop him now, before he got so big we couldn't extract him. Hazy as my mind was, I had a dim vision of my mother sanitizing a pair of chopsticks and plucking the sea horse out of me. Why not? It wasn't any bigger than a kung pao shrimp.

Ten minutes passed, and still she didn't come. I finally resorted to the lowest stratagem I could think of: I regressed seven years, and used the name I hadn't spoken since I was three. "Mommy!" I called. "Mommy, please!"

Damn it, I hadn't wanted to cry. I'd wanted to be crisp and clear: here's a medical problem, please help me fix it. Logical, like Mr. Spock, Zach's favorite TV character. But Vulcans never cry, because when you cry, your brain turns to mush. I could feel mine getting soggy now, with each cascading tear.

I didn't cry like normal people. I had prolonged, exhausting fits of sobbing—"crying jags," my mother used to call them. My chest would heave, my eyes would get so puffy I could barely see, my nose and throat would nearly swell shut. It was extremely uncomfortable but also a relief somehow. When I had to focus on trying to breathe, I couldn't think about all the things that got me crying in the first place. So the tears that were streaming down my face as I watched the minutes tick by felt very familiar. They also felt very real. Pain did not diminish for me the more that I experienced it. If anything, it increased in intensity, as if building to a crescendo that never, ever came.

Fifteen minutes that felt like five hours passed before my mother finally arrived. She stood in the doorway, backlit from the hall. She was still wearing her nurse's uniform, and the white took on a spectral glow. For once, I didn't see an angel; I saw a ghost, and the vision frightened me.

"What is it?" she asked. "I'm tired." And by God, she did look tired. Her normally erect posture was slumped, and there were circles underneath her eyes, which might just have been a trick of the light. She was only human, after all. Perhaps she'd empathize with my all-too-human frailty. Perhaps the world was a more forgiving place than I had ever realized. I began to get excited.

At last I understood the lure of confession. It wasn't about ritual, it wasn't about seduction. I'd always thought of it as a performance, but it wasn't. It was a promise: if I bare my soul to you, you'll grant me absolution. I wanted to tell my mother everything, not just about the pregnancy but all of it: my desperate struggle to be perfect, my constant fear that Daddy would leave, my wild mood swings up and down. Even the Black Beast. The words took shape inside my throat—dozens of them, hundreds, begging to be set free. But I'd been crying so long and hard by then that all that emerged was a sniffly croak. It wasn't all that I wanted to say, but in the end, it was the truth: "Mom, I'm very sick."

She sighed. "It's always something with you."

Her words went through me like a physical shock. She'd said far worse things to me in the past, but I'd never been so vulnerable before, so uncertain of reality, so willing to open up and be comforted. In spite of the evidence before my eyes, I still wasn't quite sure that the sea horse baby was actually there. I wasn't quite sure of anything, except that I needed proof at that moment that I was safe and loved. And it didn't exist. Nothing was certain, nothing was real.

I went underground, and wouldn't fully emerge again for nearly forty years. Trust is as fragile as fairies' wings and almost as hard to find. I would never fully trust another human being after that, except perhaps my father. Nor would I believe in God; I'd prayed to Him, and this was what He had delivered. At ten, I wasn't quite an atheist, but I harbored serious doubt.

I'd always been secretive—I had to be—but now I vowed to be subtle: cunning, cruel, manipulative. I'd never expose my raw and tender heart again. I'd let the world believe what it liked, but I'd never, ever let it see my flaws.

I rolled on my side to hide my swollen eyes.

"So, what is it?" my mother asked.

"My head hurts." I spoke to the wall.

"All this fuss over a little headache?" she said. "Here, let me take your pulse." She sat on my bed and took my wrist between her fingers. Looking back, I know this was a gesture of love, the best one she was capable of. But that night, her touch felt like a mockery of what a mother's love should be. "It's always something with you" was true, I knew it in my core. But that's not why it stung. I'd somehow hoped my mother would think better of me than I thought of myself.

"Perfectly normal," she said, relinquishing my wrist.

I rolled back over, reluctantly.

"Why are you crying?" she asked.

"It hurts."

"Do you want an aspirin?"

"No." I was afraid it might be bad for the baby.

"A glass of water?"

"No."

"Then what do you expect me to do?"

"Just let me sleep."

"That's probably best. Everything will look better in the morning." With that, she leaned down to kiss me on the forehead. I turned away before her lips could touch my skin.

Everything didn't look better the next morning—or the next one, or the one after that. It would be weeks before I stopped compulsively examining myself in the full-length mirror. But when the sea horse baby didn't grow an inch, and my belly didn't get any rounder, I gradually began to relax. Perhaps it had been a false alarm, or perhaps I had somehow lost the baby. But I stopped going over to Dan O'Leary's house: I told my mother I'd seen a big cockroach in their kitchen, and she immediately found somewhere else for me to stay. I also gave up climbing trees and poles.

At the college, I ignored as best I could all displays of carnal affection. I kept my hair in a neat, tight braid whenever I was on campus. And to Professor Tremaine's great consternation,

I refused to give up rhyme. It pained me to disappoint him, but I'd seen what could happen when free verse was given full rein.

Less sex, more rhyme, and I firmly believed that all would be right with the world. Finally, I thought, I was in control.

3

Days circle ever without end despite
Prayers for the consummate peace of the dead
And answers to questions undared or unsaid
Of the subtleties 'twixt black and white.

—Age thirteen

Nineteen seventy-three may have ushered in
the age of détente, but I was out of tune with the times. A
cease-fire had been agreed upon in Vietnam, and Russian
leader Leonid Brezhnev was extending a long olive branch.
But the feeling I remember most clearly from those days was
not one of peace or reconciliation. By the time I was thirteen,

I was openly at war with my mother. Adolescence had been declared.

Everything she did incensed me. Her beauty, which had always been a balm to my soul, was now a constant reminder of my own ungainly looks. I couldn't stand the way she spoke, her slight French-Canadian accent stressing diphthongs that should have remained silent. Her unconscious habit of inserting "and then he said, and then she said" into every story made me squirm with acute embarrassment in public. The tension between us got so bad that she couldn't cross the room without my finding fault with the way she swung her arms, the measure of her stride. I was constantly on edge, quivering like a cat's whiskers at a mouse hole, on alert for her next mistake.

But these were surface irritants, the sandpaper stuff of adolescence. What really made me seethe was her global view of the universe, her deeply held and sacred belief that life was out to screw you, so you'd better screw it first. Trust no one, believe in nothing. "They," whoever "they" were, were everywhere, watching and waiting for a moment's drop in vigilance. In my mother's sharp-eyed, sharp-edged world, danger lurked like germs: you might not see it, but it was always there, swarming and prolific. No wonder she made such an excellent nurse—she was hell-bent on making life antiseptic. Never rely on anyone else. Never let anyone glimpse your flaws. Never expose a naked emotion. Never, ever run barefoot in summer.

She hadn't always been like this, my father told me once. "It wasn't till after you were born," he said. "She was different with Zach. We had good times then—I used to be able to make her laugh. But then you came along, and . . ." His voice trailed off. "She never was the same again. She got nervous, and stayed that way."

I had no time for "nervous." I was thirteen, I wanted my wings. I was going places, and everyone knew it. My father insisted that I make handwritten copies of every letter I ever sent out, because he was convinced that I was going to be the first woman president, or at the very least, a Nobel Prize winner. "People will want to see your development," he said, and so I had stacks and stacks of copied letters stuffed inside my desk. I had pen pals strewn across the globe, and my correspondence ranged from popes to presidents. (When the Black Beast was in a certain kind of mood—glorious, grandiose—I felt no hesitation whatsoever at telling the leaders of the free world how I thought things ought to be run.)

Daddy's naïve belief in me would have been touching if not for the fact that Daddy trusted everyone. He believed in everything. I'd confide in him my wildest dreams, my deepest hopes, and his eyes would widen with excitement. "Where do we start?" he'd ask, and we'd soar through the stratosphere on fumes of anticipation. He was that way with the whole world, and consequently, the whole world loved to talk to him. He was born to sit on a bar stool, scotch in hand, nodding intently at strangers' stories. He listened with all of his body, his very elbows somehow alive with interest. I don't think he ever met a man he didn't like.

It's not surprising that I preferred his way of looking at things, and that the fights between my mother and me grew

increasingly frequent and more vicious. They were no longer just about whether I should wear a sweater to school that
morning because the clouds threatened rain. They were about
whether I was allowed to even believe in the possibility of a
sunny day.

It wasn't all her fault. The times were indeed a-changin':
money troubles had forced my parents to take Zach and me out
of St. Madeleine's, and Professor Tremaine had moved to the
East Coast, ending my intellectual adventures at Pomona College. Change of any kind upset me profoundly, and the transfer
to plain old public school was traumatic. Not only was I leaving
the familiar, secure embrace of the nuns who loved me, I was
forsaking the beauty of the candle-lit, incense-filled church for
the austerity of secular concrete.

Vernon Junior High School was, in a word, ugly. As I'd
learned from Dan O'Leary's penis, the Black Beast didn't like
ugly things—they made him fidget and itch. Just the sight of
them could kick off a morose mood that lasted for hours, even
days. But despite my discomfort with the aesthetics of my new
school, I still somehow managed to thrive. I was, as usual, a
cheerleader, and on the Student Council, and I made a respect-
able number of friends. I became close to one girl in particular:
Rhonda, a quick-witted gamine who, like me, was obsessed with
the rock opera *Jesus Christ Superstar* and could quote all the
lyrics verbatim. We used to take turns playing the different roles
after school. She was especially good as Jesus, while I excelled as
Mary Magdalene. I felt I understood the part.

Like the rest of my friends, Rhonda knew nothing about the

Black Beast. She attributed my many "eccentricities," as she called them, to my artistic temperament. She had a great respect for my poetry. "You'll make a wonderful writer one day," she kept insisting. I loved her for that, as much as I could love anyone at the time. Love requires a transparency of heart, and mine was clouded with shadows. We were as close as two teenage girls can be, when one of them is harboring a giant secret from the other.

I often wondered why I was fortunate enough to be one of the chosen few, one of the glorified inner circle of ten or so girls that essentially dictated fashion and feelings for the rest of the school. I was bright, but nowhere near beautiful enough. I wore braces, had small breasts, and was a bit of a klutz, forever banging into things because my head was off in the clouds somewhere. I was, however, insatiably curious, and I suppose there's no clearer pathway to popularity than genuine curiosity. When I asked someone, "How are you doing today?" it wasn't a cursory remark. I really meant it. I—or at least the writer in me—wanted to hear the whole story.

And perhaps because I was so familiar with pain myself, I could sense it in others instinctively. Then, as now, I could take one look into a person's eyes and know if there was trouble brewing inside, no matter how hard he or she tried to hide it. I had the two traits essential to a born confidante: empathy and the ability to keep a secret. I'd been practicing secrecy my entire life.

But the balms of popularity ended at school; they didn't soothe the increasingly uncomfortable situation at home. I tried to escape into literature, but even my discovery of Jane Austen and her neatly bounded little world couldn't drown out

the discord from our living room. My parents had dropped all
pretense of not arguing in front of the kids. Now, as soon as my
father got home, it was money this and money that, and how are
we going to pay all these goddamned bills?

Up until then, so far as I could tell, we'd been doing relatively fine. Both my parents had to work hard to support us, but
we lived in a nice house at the end of a pretty cul-de-sac, with
a big backyard and a swimming pool. Sure, my parents would
argue about money sometimes; whose parents didn't? But it was
nothing like this—this snarling, snapping sound of desperation.
Something bad had happened to put us in this dire financial
state. It would be years before I finally learned what that was,
and even then, the details were murky.

All I knew at the time was that my father was commuting
back and forth to Ventura, a good four-hour drive each day.
He was building a tract of homes on a speculative project he
called Wonderland Hill, financed God knows how—mostly
by his optimism and charisma, I suspect. One of these homes
was going to be our new dream house. It was enormous, and
Zach and I got to plan our own rooms from scratch. Mine
had a wraparound picture window, with built-in bookcases
and a sweeping view of the as-yet-undefiled greens and grays
of Aliso Canyon. It was the perfect vista for a budding writer:
undiscovered territory. It's no coincidence that I spent the rest
of my life searching for that canyon view, and once I found one
that resembled it, I stayed put.

We were going to be happy there on Wonderland Hill. I knew it in my bones. Zach knew it, my father knew it—even my mother, who never allowed an elated thought to pass through her brain undissected, thought it might be possible. I was only thirteen, but I was already weary of the way things were and was wise enough to realize that life offers you only so many fresh beginnings. On Wonderland Hill, my parents wouldn't fight. My mother and I would bake oatmeal cookies together, wearing matching aprons. Zach would come out of his room and be eager to play. And the Black Beast wouldn't bedevil me anymore—he'd be so distracted by the move, he'd forget that I existed.

It was strange: even though it meant relocating to a brand-new city, starting a new school, and making all new friends, Wonderland Hill didn't frighten me. It wasn't change; it was reclamation.

What I couldn't foresee, and what I'll never forget, was the night that my father didn't come home. We waited at dinner for him—I remember the ice-cold mashed potatoes, and how hard it was to force them down. My mother wasn't much of a cook, but she made excellent mashed potatoes: dense and smooth and creamy. But that night, there was a lump in my throat, and it was difficult to swallow.

Traffic on the 101 Freeway could be brutal, so it wasn't completely unusual that my father would sometimes miss a meal. But he always stopped off at a gas station and called to say he'd be late. That night, though, we heard nothing—just the dial tone when I checked the phone to make sure that it was working.

By midnight, my mother was frantic. I had an exam the next
morning, and she tried to make me go to bed, but no way was
I going to close my eyes without knowing that Daddy was safe.
My parents hadn't been fighting any more than usual lately, so I
couldn't imagine why he hadn't at least called. Zach, bless him,
tried to be the man of the house. "I'll wait up for him," he told
us. "You guys go to bed." But although I agreed to put on my
pajamas, by two in the morning we were all still wide awake and
wondering. Zach had called the highway patrol by then: no ac-
cidents on the 101. My mother called all the hospitals she could
think of between home and Ventura. No one resembling my
father's description had been admitted that night.

Finally, as a sliver of sunrise shot between the blinds, the
telephone rang. I was the first to pounce.

"Daddy?"

"Put your mother on." No "sweetie," no "baby," no explanation.

"I was so worried," I started to say, but he interrupted me.

"*Now*, damn it."

It was the first time my father had ever sworn at me, and I
was frightened. His voice sounded odd—tight and cold, as if
someone had him by the throat and was strangling all the natural warmth out of him.

I handed my mother the phone.

"Jack, where on earth—" She stopped, and I watched the
blood drain from her face. "Wait, let me get a pen. Okay." She
scribbled something down. "I'll be there as soon as I can." Then
she hung up and turned to face Zach and me. Her eyes were

as chilly as my father's voice had been, but there was a strange gleam of satisfaction behind them.

"Your father had a flat tire," she said. "I have to go get him. No school today. Zach, you're in charge."

"But why didn't he—" I tried to ask.

"Did you hear me? Your brother's in charge." With that, she grabbed her purse and was out the door before I could say another word.

"Zach, what's going on?" For once, I was glad of his eagle eye. He was closer to my mother than I was. Sometimes he even invited her into his room, and they would talk together for hours. Surely he would know why she was so obviously lying.

"I can't tell you," he said with a self-important look on his face.

"Oh, balls. You just don't know."

"I know a lot more than you think I do."

"Come on, Zach, please. Is something wrong with Daddy?"

"You're his pet. Why don't you ask him?"

There was a sneer in his voice, but something deeper too. I could tell that he'd been wounded. It wasn't always easy for him that my father and I were so close, and the Black Beast demanded so much attention. For a moment, I felt guilty, but then I shrugged it off. I couldn't help it if I was Daddy's little girl. Besides, Zach was clearly my mother's favorite, and I didn't let it get to me. Or at least, I didn't hold it against Zach.

He turned to go back to his room, but not without a parting shot. "I can tell you one thing," he said. "You're not getting that picture window."

I grabbed him by the arm and looked up at him, pleading. At sixteen, Zach was already well on his way to his full adult height of six foot two, and I had to crank back my neck to see in his eyes. What I saw there unnerved me. He was scared too. I wanted to wrap both my arms around him and hold him tight, at least until his eyes got back to normal and I felt like I could breathe again. But Zach and I never touched like that. For once, I wished we weren't brother and sister. I wished that we were friends.

He shook me off and went down the hall, shutting his door firmly behind him. I wandered around the living room, picking things up and putting them down. I ran my hands over the keys of the organ and tried to coax out a tune: "You Are My Sunshine," Daddy's favorite.

"Stop that!" Zach shouted from inside his room. He was, of course, right. It was my mother's precious organ, and we weren't supposed to touch it when she wasn't home.

It was a curious thing, that instrument—a monument to my mother's thrift. Although she lived in abject terror of spending an unexamined cent, that didn't keep her from spending money. She just spent it in odd, miserly ways. In five years, she'd supposedly hoarded enough nickels, dimes, and quarters under her bed to buy that organ. Why she wanted it, I never knew. She didn't play; none of us did. And of course, in her opinion, there was never enough money for lessons. So the organ simply sat there: a constant reminder to all of us of the essential importance of pocket change.

My father needed that reminder. If my mother was a

clenched fist when it came to money, Daddy was an open hand. He spent money reflexively, like breathing. It didn't matter what he was buying—shoelaces, a summer house, a dry gin martini—he always wanted the best, not just for himself but for all of us. And especially for me. All a canny salesman ever had to do was invoke that magic incantation, "It's the best," and my father was sold.

Somehow, despite how broke my mother claimed we were, Daddy always had a nickel for an ice-cream cone. When he was home, he'd treat the whole neighborhood. The instant the Good Humor truck tinkled down our street, he was the first one out the door, pockets overflowing with coins. Every now and then, I'd wonder where he got all that ready change, and if the sacred hoard beneath my mother's bed had actually been violated. But my parents slept in separate bedrooms, and my mother kept her door securely locked during the day, so plunder seemed unlikely.

My curiosity about the source of my father's wealth never lasted much longer than my Fudgsicle. It never really mattered to me if Daddy's gains were ill-gotten or not. "You deserve the best," he told me, and who was I to argue with the wisest man I ever knew?

Where in God's name could he be?

It wasn't until well after three in the afternoon that I finally heard the sound I'd been longing for: the scratch of his key in the lock. I ran to the front door and threw my arms around him,

burying my face in his shirt. It took a few moments to register—
he didn't smell like Daddy, crisp and clean and familiar. He
smelled musty and dark, like someone who'd been smoking too
many cigarettes in too small a room. I wrinkled my nose and
looked up at his face. It was a shock: my father was always neat
and clean-shaven. He prided himself on the closeness of his
shave, as I knew from the many mornings I'd spent watching
him wield his old-fashioned straight-edge razor. The man I had
my arms around had a day's worth of stubble on his chin, and
there was a dried streak of something across his left cheek.

But the biggest shock of all was when he looked away. He
wouldn't meet my eyes. All the questions I'd been dying to ask
him evaporated in that moment. I knew then what that strange
smell was: it was shame, and I was all too familiar with that.

So I didn't say a word, just hugged him tighter and tighter,
until he finally stepped back. "I'm tired," he said. "I'm going to
go wash up and rest before dinner."

It was a dinner that I wouldn't soon forget. I kept waiting for
someone to say something, anything, about what had happened.
When my brother asked, a bit more politely than usual, "Please
pass the mashed potatoes," I wanted to grab the whole bowl
and chuck it at him. I wasn't really mad at Zach; for a change,
I wasn't even mad at my mother, and certainly not at my father,
who looked so tired he could barely chew. Nausea swam in my
stomach. I was sick to death of the sight of them. Sick to death
of swallowing when what I really wanted to do was shout, "What
the hell is going on?"

Surely this was not how other people did things at their

houses. I thought of my friend Maria and her gabbling, squabbling family. You could barely get a word in edgewise there. Everybody knew everything about everyone else and never stopped talking about it for a minute. Why couldn't we be more like them? I looked down at my dinner plate. The gravy was threatening to run off my potatoes and invade the sanctity of my roast beef. I quickly put up a barrier of peas between them. There, that felt better. Everything in its place. Nothing touching anything else.

I took a careful bite of the beef. It needed salt, but the shaker was way over past Zach, and I was afraid to open my mouth to ask for it, afraid of what might come tumbling out. The words were nearly choking me, but I gulped them down, along with the tasteless meat. Fine. I could live without salt. What I couldn't live without was answers. But the man I'd always turned to for answers was now a cipher himself.

Not for the first time in my young life, I thought of Sherlock Holmes. What would he do? He was always faced with mysteries, and he always figured them out. I knew his methods: "Eliminate the impossible, and whatever remains, however improbable, must be the truth." I would deduce from the evidence before me where my father had spent the night.

I snuck a glance at him. His hair was neatly combed now, the stubble gone, but he looked glum and tired. My mother was always accusing him of having affairs with everyone he came into contact with: the waitress, the bank teller, the girl at the supermarket checkout, and of course, the mysterious Rebecca. There wasn't a woman alive she wasn't suspicious of, including but not limited to my own friend Janie, who had developed a little earlier than the rest of us girls. But surely if Daddy was having an affair, he would look more satisfied; or at least he would make a greater pretense of being solicitous to my mother, to cover up his tracks. As it was, I hadn't heard them exchange a single word since he had come back home.

I snuck another glance, this time at my mother. She didn't have the old familiar "He's-cheating-on-me" scowl on her face. Instead there was a smug "I-told-you-so" look in her eyes. What had she been accusing him of lately, besides the usual infidelity? It had to be money. And then it came flooding back to me: their argument last Saturday night. I'd come in early from my ballet class to find them in the thick of it—my mother furious, waving her arms at my father, who sat stone-faced and silent in his brown leather chair. "That's what you get when you deal with people like that," she said. Then she saw me and clammed up. I thought it was rather strange at the time, because normally she would have just kept on arguing. I'd meant to ask Zach about it, but I forgot.

Was it possible that my father was dealing with bad people? Eliminate the impossible, and whatever remains, however improbable . . . Not only was it possible, it was highly likely, given his willingness to trust in anyone, anytime, even the most obvious snake oil salesman. No doubt the bad guys had told him their stuff was "the best."

I felt sick again. Bad people meant trouble, maybe even jail. And sure enough, there was a livid bruise along the side of my father's wrist, where handcuffs might have hurt him. Sherlock

Holmes would undoubtedly have been proud of me, but I took no comfort from my cleverness. How was I ever to know for sure? The sheer weight of all the unconfirmed suspicions I carried around with me was like molten lead in my veins.

Suddenly I was exhausted. My hand felt so heavy, I couldn't lift the fork. I wasn't even hungry anymore. I just wanted to go to bed and stay there for days, because bed was the only safe corner in the house—the only one that didn't pose unanswerable questions. I dared to raise my eyes from my plate and look at the silent faces around me. What were they thinking? Were they all aching for answers too? If I opened my mouth and spoke the unspeakable, what was the very worst that could happen?

No, no, never. I'd been through an earthquake before, and I knew: something fragile would be shattered.

So I kept my mouth shut and continued to pick at my food, because that's how secrets were treated in our house: with exquisite inattention. It must have been the right prescription, because they flourished like the scarlet bougainvillea that ran along the back fence. We each had our own special variety. Mine, of course, was my struggle with the Black Beast, my knowledge that I was so different inside from the way I looked, I was practically two separate people. Zach's life was shrouded in mystery too: just what did he do in his room all day, and why would he not come out to play?

My mother's secret was even murkier. Something bad must have happened to her, sometime, somewhere, to make her so afraid of life. I'd asked her about it often enough, not in a nice way but with the nastiness of a thirteen-year-old exasperated by her every move: "Mom, what's the matter with you?" But she was not one for introspection. The most I ever got out of her was the stone story.

Apparently, when she was a little girl, she was a dead ringer for the young Shirley Temple. Her mother dressed her up and curled her hair to accentuate the resemblance. Although she lived in a small farming village just outside the quiet backwaters of Windsor, she attracted a lot of notice.

Her friends didn't like it. One day when she was stumbling home from school through the snow, a gang of girls stepped out from behind a tree and began taunting her, pulling her ringlets, tearing her dress. She started to run, but they followed her, pelting her from behind with stones and debris. The only blemish on my mother's body—a small, triangular scar on the back of her calf—came from that attack.

When she finally made it home to the farm, sobbing and terrified, she ran to find her father. He was sitting in his rocking chair, packing a pipe. This is the only strong visual memory I have of my grandfather: a lean, almost gaunt figure, sitting in his rocking chair, silhouetted against a dark, wintry window. Picture Whistler's mother as a man, and you've got him. My mother always called him a saint, but to me he was a forbidding presence—a man of few words, each one carefully chosen.

After my mother finished telling him what had happened, my grandfather brushed the dirt off her Red Riding Hood cloak (just like the one Shirley Temple used to wear) and looked at her through a wreath of smoke. "You asked for attention. You got it," he said. Out of this, my mother concocted a moral: "Don't ever be too pretty," she used to tell me, stroking the hair back out of my eyes. "People will throw stones at you."

I'm sure there were many more stories like this, but my mother never told them to me. For the most part, she flat-out refused to talk about her childhood.

"Why do you want to know that?" she'd ask.

"I'm curious," I'd say.

"You're nosy," she'd counter. "It's nobody's business but my own."

The vigilance with which she guarded her past made me all the more certain that there were dark, brutal incidents lurking back there that had made her who she was. In rare moments of compassion, I wondered if maybe she even had her own Black Beast to contend with. It would certainly explain her mercurial moods, the sudden, volatile flare-ups of temper that whipped through the house like a devil wind, leaving us all breathless and shaken.

But up until the night he didn't come home, I was sure that my father had no secrets from me. I felt like I knew his home-town of McCracken, Kansas, as well as if I'd grown up there myself. It helped that it was the town in which the movie *Paper Moon* was filmed. When I was thirteen, Daddy and I sat through that picture three times in a row. "There, that's the front stoop where I used to drink pop," he said. "There's the silo, there's the Methodist Church, and just around the corner is where we lived." McCracken was such a sparse, dusty town, its one main drag barely as long as a sneeze, I felt sure there were no secrets there. Where could they hide them?

In the end, that's why I never asked my father to explain his
whereabouts that awful night. It was partly respect but mostly
self-indulgence: I didn't want to know his shame. Shame would
have been a smudge on the page. For all my love of great literature, with its tragic heroes and complex plots, I preferred my
gods pristine.

It wasn't until many years later, when I was in my thirties,
that my mother finally let it slip: "Remember the night your father spent in jail?" she said. I tried to grill her—I was a lawyer by
then, and pretty good at grilling—but she refused to give. The
only thing I could ferret out was that several of the contractors
my father had hired were alleged to be in league with the Mafia.
That's all she knew, or all she'd tell me.

I assume that because there was no trial, and I never heard
anything further about it, my father was eventually acquitted
of all charges. But the allegations took their toll: whatever had
actually happened that night, it was the end of Wonderland Hill.
Then began the lean times, the bad times, the times I'd rather
not write about: the reign of Brew 102.

My father couldn't get a job. No doubt because of the cloud
hanging over his reputation, no one in the construction industry
would hire him. He tried retail for a while, selling mobile homes
out of a tiny trailer, chain-smoking his way through the empty
days. But the economy wouldn't cooperate, and his heart truly
wasn't in it. He had a dream—"a vision," he called it—of yet
another project. I remember the night he told us about it. *The*

Wonderful World of Disney was on TV, and it was just at that moment when Tinker Bell flies in to light up the screen.

"I've had an inspiration," he announced. "By this time five years from now—maybe three, if I'm lucky—we're all going to be millionaires."

My mother rolled her eyes and looked at Zach, who shrugged and went back to fiddling with an assortment of bolts and screws he had spread out all over the floor. I was all ears.

"Tell me, tell me," I said.

"The problem with Wonderland Hill," Daddy said, "was that it didn't suit the times. Everything was too big. Too many rooms, too much upkeep. People don't want all that responsibility; there's too much on their minds these days. They don't want more, they want less. So I'm going to give them less, and we're going to make a fortune."

Zach snorted, and I looked daggers at him. "Shut up, Daddy's talking."

"You don't believe me, Zach?" Daddy said. "Tell me, what do you think of your car?"

Zach's eyes lit up, the way they always did when anyone mentioned that hunk of junk. For his sixteenth birthday, my parents had given him a used Volkswagen Beetle—not just any old bug, but one with a Rolls-Royce grille attached to the front and a fake bar behind the back seat. Zach was as proud of that thing as if it had been an actual Rolls. He spent hours every day waxing it, polishing the metal, tinkering with the engine. When he wasn't in his room, we knew where we could find him: in the garage, under the car, in his heaven.

"It's the best," Zach said.

"It's the best because it's small," Daddy said. "Nobody wants huge gas guzzlers anymore, what with the oil crisis and all. Times are uncertain, people don't want to be surrounded by all that extra space. They want to feel cocooned."

"My teacher, Mrs. Gayle, told us the universe is shrinking," I said, trying to be helpful.

"Mrs. Gayle is a very wise woman. Everything is shrinking. You mark my words, small is where the next big money is." Daddy got up and went to his desk. He scribbled something on a piece of paper and handed it to me. "Go show that to your mother."

On the page, in my father's neat, slanted handwriting, was a single word: "Volkshouse."

She looked at it and shook her head. "No. No more big ideas."

"But that's just it," my father said. "Nothing about it is big. It will be stripped to the bones—just as much house as is needed for a single family starting out. Not a centimeter more."

I cottoned to the idea instantly. "You mean, just like Zach's car, except without the Rolls-Royce front and the bar in the back."

"Exactly. And I know the perfect place to build them: that long stretch of desert between here and Palm Springs, out by Victorville. Nobody's thought of developing that area yet. Lots will go for a song."

I felt a slight twinge of fear. The desert was ugly. And heat sometimes drove the Black Beast mad. But I would never let my father see my hesitation. "Brilliant!" I said. "And when we make our first million, can we go to London and stay at the Savoy Hotel?" A steady diet of Jane Austen had turned me into a rabid Anglophile.

"You bet, honey. And Paris too. Whichever hotel you choose."

"The Ritz?"

"If you like."

"In a suite?"

"Of course."

My mother got up, crumpled the sheet of paper, and tossed it onto the coffee table. "While you two are planning your Grand Tour, I'm going to go make the sandwiches for tomorrow. What do you think, Zach? Bologna sound good?"

"Bologna sounds perfect," Zach said, grinning. "And don't forget the caviar."

I hated it when Zach and my mother ganged up together. I could feel the Black Beast stirring, especially when I saw the crestfallen look on Daddy's face. I knew that I should get up and go to my room, but the urge to say something, do something, protest somehow, was just too powerful. I tried to wait it out, but already my hands were twitching, my eyes darting about the room, looking for something to throw.

Throwing things always made me feel better. The Black Beast especially liked smashing glass; the shattering sound was so soothing. But there was no glassware in reach, so I did the next best thing. I grabbed a handful of Zach's carefully sorted bolts and screws and pitched them at him as hard as I could.

One of the metal pieces was sharp and nearly sliced him in the eye. A tiny trickle of blood ran down his cheekbone.

"You're a freaking nutcase," Zach said, and he raised his hand to smack me. My father grabbed his arm.

"You know the rules. No hitting in this house."

"But she—"

"Terri Lynn, what have we told you about throwing things? Apologize to your brother immediately."

"I'm sorry," I mumbled. The Black Beast was fully aroused by then, but I wouldn't directly disobey my father's order.

"You go straight to your room," my mother said, pulling a handkerchief out of her pocket. "And you—" She whirled and faced my father. "What do you think you're doing, getting her all riled up like that? You know she believes every word you say."

I longed to scratch and claw at her, to make blood run down her face the way it was still trickling down Zach's. But I wouldn't do it in front of Daddy. I restrained myself to words. "Leave him alone! It's a great idea, and you're just too stupid to see it."

"You shouldn't speak to your mother like that," my father said. His voice was soft but firm. "But it *is* a great idea, Julia."

"They're all great ideas. And what are we supposed to live on in the meantime? Pixie dust? You just sit around all day and come up with these grand schemes, and I'm supposed to work my fingers to the bone while you—"

"Stop it!" I shouted. "Can't you see what you're doing to him?" My father was leaning his head back on the couch, all the excitement puffed out of him.

"Go to your room this instant, or I'll—" I didn't let her finish.

I slammed the den door behind me. I already knew this scenario by heart. Without me around to argue about, my parents would turn on each other, while poor Zach continued to bleed. I'd heard their argument so many times, I could have recited it as easily as the Lord's Prayer. My mother was furious that she'd had to take the night shift at the hospital because it paid more, while my father "sat around all day and dreamed," waiting for a construction-related job to materialize. The kicker was always this: my mother knew someone who knew someone who knew of a job down at Brew 102.

I don't know why the words "Brew 102" conjured up such fear in me, but to this day, they still do. It was just a brewery, after all. A big, sprawling, smoking factory right off the freeway, a few miles past Skid Row. We'd passed it many times on our way to nicer places. I think it may have been the ugliest place I'd ever seen, and the thought of my father disappearing into that grimy, billowing murk frightened me to the core. I was afraid he'd never emerge again — or worse yet, he would emerge a different man, no longer the pure white soul that I loved.

The men who worked at Brew 102 didn't wear crisply tailored pin-striped shirts that smelled of aftershave. They didn't carry neat leather briefcases filled with architectural drawings. They surely didn't kiss their little girls good-bye with light and happy hearts, knowing that they were off to do what they loved doing best.

I'd seen them. The men who worked at Brew 102 wore thick, greasy overalls the color of chimney soot and carried big metal cylinders that looked as if they could snap a man's back in two.

They trudged, one after the other, like prisoners on a chain gang, each step heavier than the last.

Maybe I understood innocence better than my mother did, because I was closer to it at thirteen. But if I knew one thing, it was that Brew 102 meant more than just my father working at a job he couldn't stand. It meant the death of dreams.

I knew he would someday capitulate. Nobody could withstand my mother on a mission. And as I had feared, everything changed after that. There was no more poetry in the evenings — Daddy comfortably settled in with his nightcap, me with my latest attempt at a sonnet. He was dead tired by the time he came home. His face was streaked with sweat, and he stunk, quite frankly, like cat piss. Much as I loved him, even I found it difficult to hug him when he walked through the front door.

I blamed my mother for all of this. Granted, I wasn't the one having to put food on the table or worry about the bills. In hindsight, it's easy to see that of course we couldn't survive on one income, and of course my father had to get some kind of job. But why this one, which leached all the color out of his face and left him so catatonic at dinner?

It was a bad time to be broke. The ongoing Watergate scandal had cast serious doubt on President Nixon's ability to focus on economic policy, and inflation was spiraling out of control — the highest it had been in two decades. The dollar was shrinking, the stock market plummeting, and the threat of recession was on everyone's lips. According to Daddy, the construction business was particularly hard-hit: steel and lumber were fixed at exorbitant prices, and high interest rates decreased the availability of loans. It was the first time in my life that I couldn't have everything I wanted. Now, when my mother said we were "too poor to afford a bag of potato chips," I actually believed her.

Even if I didn't know the clinical term for the cloud that hung over our house, I was so familiar with the way it felt that I didn't need a word to describe it. It was as if the Black Beast, in one of his fouler moods, had escaped my body and infected everyone else. Bleak, dark, listless, and cold, the days dragged on with no end in sight. Oddly enough, though, the sight of everyone else's depression didn't trigger one of my own. Quite the contrary: I was agitated, excited, on the move. I felt galvanized, as if I had a new purpose in life. I'm ashamed to say just what that was, although at the time I thought it was a noble calling: I intended to reinvent our family, with me as the loving, nurturing mother.

I was already well on my way to usurping her. Ever since I was a child, whenever we went on a family drive, I would sit in the front seat, next to my father. My mother was relegated to the back seat with Zach. She fumed about this, but I was adamant. I had to sit up front with Daddy, or else I wouldn't get in the car. She put up with this to avoid triggering a tantrum, because my tantrums were horrific. When I was younger, they took the form of explosions: I would scream, kick, bite anything at hand, and bang my head against the sidewalk until I got my own way.

I grew subtler as I got older. By thirteen, I knew the value of a venomous whisper. "He's going to leave you one day, you know,"

I'd say to my mother, under my breath. "You already sleep in separate bedrooms. As soon as you stop being pretty, he's gone. Are you sure you want to make a scene?" She'd be so shocked, she'd get into the back seat without arguing—anything to shut me up, I suspect.

I continued my insidious campaign at dinner. Now that my mother worked the night shift, it was just Daddy and Zach and me, and Zach would leave the table as soon as possible to get back under his car. That left me alone with my father, his head drooping over the mashed potatoes—the one thing I ever learned how to cook from my mother.

When the Black Beast wanted to, he could coax words from a stone. I'd tilt my head and fire up my eyes until they sparkled with curiosity. "Tell me more about the Volkshouse," I'd say.

"I'm too tired," he'd mumble. I never let that dissuade me.

"It reminds me of 'Goldilocks,'" I'd say. "Not too much house, not too little. Just right. And everybody gets a happy ending. How many rooms do you think that would take?"

At first, he'd answer me with monosyllables. But eventually, as I kept peppering him with questions, his enthusiasm for the project would reignite. After a few weeks, he started to sketch some ideas on his napkin. That progressed to legal pads, until finally, one night he got out the blueprint paper, and I knew that we were home free.

Those were glorious nights, that stretched into the wee hours of the morning. Just Daddy and me, the way it was supposed to be. Every once in a while, on his way to his room, Zach would poke his head in the door to see what we were doing. "We're working," I'd say, and I'd shoo him off to bed. And work we did: long, hard hours of musing and measuring, Daddy downing endless cups of the Folgers I'd fix for him. I didn't need coffee, and I didn't need sleep. I had the Black Beast to fuel me, and his enthusiasm never once waned.

I quickly learned the tools of my father's trade until I was as good as a surgical nurse to him. "Hand me the protractor," he'd say, or the compass, or the triangle. "Beveled or fluorescent?" I'd ask, and I'd slap the right one into his palm. I learned the difference between the ebony sketching pencil and the seven-millimeter drafting pencil; the Pink Pearl eraser versus the Magic Rub. I memorized all the myriad templates: for lettering, landscape design, master ellipses, and my favorite, the lavatory planning template, with its cute little cutouts of toilets and sinks. I stood at his side, eraser at the ready, both of us ensconced in the warm halo of the magnifying lamp. I refilled his coffee before it got cold, trying to anticipate his every desire.

I was there before he realized he needed me.

We kept "the project" secret from my mother, of course. She never would have let me stay up so late, especially on school nights. I'm not sure why my father allowed it, and for so many months in a row. Every now and again he'd say, "Are you sure you aren't tired? You really need to get to bed." But I'd shake my head and say something like, "Don't you think the toilet's a little too close to the door?" and we'd be off and drafting again. How was he to know that lack of sleep kept the Black Beast in a state of constant arousal?

My late nights never impaired my performance at school. In

fact, with the Black Beast kicked up into high gear, I excelled even more at public school than I had at St. Madeleine's. Although I was getting only a few hours of sleep every night, my energy seemed boundless, my ambitions unlimited. The Black Beast simply would not close his eyes. He just kept driving me on and on, to fill up every empty moment with action and acclaim.

I continued to get straight As, of course, but I also had a finger in every extracurricular pie. In addition to my ongoing tap, ballet, and baton lessons, cheerleading practice, and Student Council duties, I directed the school play: a silly Western in which I also starred as Lydia Sagebrush, a feisty cowgirl whom I conceived as a cross between Marlene Dietrich and Mae West. "Stop vamping the audience!" the drama coach kept scolding me. I obeyed her up until opening night, when the Black Beast couldn't stand it anymore and let loose with a volley of head tosses, hip thrusts, broad winks, and knowing smiles. The review in the school paper was actually quite good—but then, if memory serves me, I wrote it.

On top of all this, I took my homework quite seriously. When Mrs. Gayle told us to memorize a short poem and recite it the next week in English class, I ignored the "short" part and went straight to the Master. Most of the students came back with familiar doggerel, along the lines of "I think that I shall never see / A poem as lovely as a tree." I marched in wearing my witch's hat from Halloween and carrying my mother's best Crock Pot, which was filled with dry ice that billowed, I hoped, like fog on a blasted heath. I can still remember the dumbfounded looks on the faces of the students and Mrs. Gayle as I launched into act 4, scene 1 of Shakespeare's *Macbeth*: "Double, double, toil and trouble / Fire burn and cauldron bubble . . ."

Vernon Junior High didn't quite know what to make of me.

As always, I judged my well-being by my accomplishments. I never stopped to consider the toll this relentless pace was taking on my body. I didn't have any desire to eat: chewing felt like a waste of time that could be spent on more productive things. The few hours that I managed to sleep, I sweat straight through the sheets. But sleep was for sissies, I thought, and what did it matter if I lost a few more pounds off my already skinny frame? I just wore looser clothes to hide it. So what if I had circles the color of bruised plums underneath my eyes, and my skin looked dull and ashen? Daddy was finally happy again, and that made me feel beautiful inside, no matter what the mirror said.

Professor Tremaine's untimely departure for the East Coast had left me bereft, bored, and much too overeducated for my own good. The boredom part was dangerous, since the Black Beast craved constant stimulation. Most of the time, I made up my own mischief—like the time I picked up a scruffy old copy of *Das Kapital* at the Salvation Army and tried to convert the entire seventh grade to Communism. Although the Cold War was beginning to thaw in 1973, in our little nook of middle-class society, *Communism* was still a virulent word.

While I can't say I truly understood Marx's theory, his anger at the oppression of the working classes came through loud and clear, and it touched a tender nerve in me. I was ticked off that Zach had just had his allowance raised, even though I felt I did more chores around the house, and far more conscientiously than he did. (He was older, my father explained, and had more expenses.) Plus I'd wanted a new bike for ages and was sick to death of hearing why "the economy" wouldn't allow it. Capitalism clearly wasn't working anymore; at least not at 1555 North Elm Court. Revolution was long overdue.

Whenever the Black Beast had a passion about something, I figured the whole world must share it. I didn't realize that in their entire lives, most people never felt as intensely as I did on an ordinary Tuesday afternoon. I made up a slew of flyers proclaiming "Down with Tyranny!" "Utopia Now!" and other such vague rabble-rousing phrases. I handed them out at school the next day, exhorting the students to "Unite for a Classless Society!" I'm not sure they understood what I meant by that, but the timing was perfect. Without consulting the Student Council, the teachers had recently cut fifteen minutes off our lunch period and eliminated the afternoon recess altogether. Everyone was peeved, especially those kids who needed the quick secret hit of nicotine that the three o'clock break had provided.

Maybe teenagers are just plain trigger-happy when it comes to taunting authority. In any event, my idea took off, and by the end of that day, we were all calling each other "comrade." My hot-pink flyers were plastered everywhere: on lockers, on the windows of the teachers' lounge, and all across the "Do Not Post Flyers Here!" sign on the boiler room. That night, two teachers' homes were allegedly covered with pink toilet paper. I deny any complicity in this; nor will I rat out my fellow revolutionaries.

The next morning, the unthinkable happened: I was called into the principal's office. The memory of that long walk behind the hall monitor still makes me shudder. My footsteps resounded in the empty corridors. I had a blister on one heel from breaking in my new tap shoes, and the cruel, hard concrete tortured my feet. There was a pep rally scheduled for later that day, so I was wearing my cheerleading uniform. I wished that the skirt was a little bit longer, to hide the quivering gooseflesh on my legs.

Mrs. Murgatroyd, the principal's assistant, raised an eyebrow. "I must say, I'm a little surprised to see *you* here," she said. "Go in and wait. He'll be back soon."

I went in and waited. And waited. Waiting was not one of the Black Beast's strengths. I grew increasingly anxious, which wasn't good. Fear often manifested as arrogance in me, and I was in enough trouble already.

"It's a tactic," the Black Beast kept whispering. "The son of a bitch is keeping you waiting just to make you sweat."

"Shut up," I told him. "Let me handle this. I'm better with authority than you are."

But the Beast simply couldn't sit still. After five minutes, I got up and paced, ignoring the pain from my blister. By the time Principal Griggs finally arrived, I'd worked myself up into a lather of righteous indignation.

He was a short man who compensated with a big, booming voice. He never needed a microphone in the auditorium, nor did he need to say things twice. You got him the first time.

"Is this your handiwork?" he bellowed, brandishing a flyer.

Loud noises always unnerved me, but I was prepared. "I hereby invoke my Fifth Amendment right against self-incrimination," I said.

"So it *was* you. What on earth's gotten into you?"

I talked faster. "Every student has a right to free speech under the First Amendment, and a right to petition against injustice, and—"

"Not on my boiler room, they don't," he said. He opened up my file and leafed through it, shaking his head. "What do you know about those TP parties last night?" he asked.

"I invoke my Fifth—"

"Yes, yes, I know." He sat back into his chair, steepled his fingers, and looked at me over them. "Parents have been calling me all morning, complaining that their kids won't do their chores because it's exploitation of cheap labor. You disrupted an entire day's schoolwork. Not to mention that the glue you used won't come off the windows of the teachers' lounge. Technically, I have no choice but to suspend you."

I was torn between terror and outrage. I thought of the look on my father's face when he heard of my disgrace, and terror won out.

"Please, sir, you can't suspend me."

"Give me one good reason why."

"My father."

"He'll kill you?"

"No. It will kill him."

He looked surprised. Then he did the last thing I expected.

He softened his voice and said, "You don't quite fit in here, do you?"

His question cut me to the quick. I'd never fit in anywhere, but I didn't think it showed. On the surface, I looked like a winner: cheerleaders had to be popular, just by definition, right? But I knew the façade was shallow and easily pierced. At Vernon Junior High, as at St. Madeleine's, I had a great many friends but few intimates. And even the kids I was closest to—even Rhonda, my very best girlfriend—didn't know about the Black Beast.

"What do you mean?" I asked, struggling to keep my voice steady.

"Well, I see here in your file that you come to us from St. Madeleine's by way of Pomona College—quite impressive, by the way—and that you've received nothing but glowing reports from all your teachers about your schoolwork. With the caveat that some of your teachers wish you'd stop correcting them in front of the class."

I lowered my head. I did have a bad habit of doing that, but then, so many of the teachers just didn't know how to spell.

"Look at me."

I raised my head.

"Here's what I see when I look at you. You look exhausted. There are dark circles under your eyes, and your hands keep twitching. You've got a near-perfect record on paper, but I get the sense that something's not right. Tell me, dear, what's wrong with you?"

Few things in my life have ever hurt so bad as that single word, *dear*. I heard echoes of my mother's proclamation

"There's something wrong with her," and I wondered if those words would chase me the rest of my life.

Principal Griggs looked tired as well. There was a slight sheen of sweat on his high, balding forehead, and for a moment I thought of offering him my handkerchief, but then I remembered there were no pockets in my cheerleading skirt. The window behind him was open to catch the breeze, and I heard the sound of someone drilling on a nearby street. Going deeper, deeper. Exposing the core. Fixing whatever was wrong, so the world could start out fresh again.

I can't say I wasn't tempted.

The Black Beast erupted inside me. He wasn't my mother's child for nothing—he knew when he was being threatened. If I exposed him, if I could somehow even find the words to describe him to Principal Griggs, "they" would make him go away.

"Fuck you" bubbled up to my lips, and it took all my self-discipline to break out into a fit of coughing instead. I coughed until my face turned red, and tears streamed from my eyes. The tears were about far more than the cough, but only I could tell.

"Do you want a glass of water?" He nodded at the Sparkletts bottle in the corner.

By the time I'd filled a Dixie cup and drunk it down—not easy, my hands were trembling so—I managed to compose myself. Secrets were secret for a very good reason: they looked too hideous in the light. I knew how ugly the Black Beast was. By now he was a mass of ulcerous sores from constant irritation; no doubt he would stink in the open air. Better to keep him hidden away, enshrouded in the dark.

Let the drillers drill. I wasn't ready.

"Thank you, sir," I said as politely as possible, "but I invoke the Fifth."

He sighed. "All right. I think what's going on here, which is unbelievable given all that you're already doing, is that you've got too much spare time on your hands. In light of your otherwise exemplary record, I'm not going to suspend you. But I am going to make you perform some community service. And you're going to scrub that boiler room until it's spotless."

I nearly jumped up and kissed his bald forehead. "Thank you for your clemency."

"Clemency." He smiled. "Excellent word."

I pushed it. "And you won't tell my father about this?"

"No, *you* are going to tell your father. I want you to promise me that, or no deal."

Even the Black Beast had to admit: this guy was good. The last thing in the world I would normally agree to do was tell my father I'd misbehaved. Sully his perfect image of me as his ideal little girl? Never. But there were far more dangerous things lurking in that office: compassion and a keen eye. I had to get the hell out of there.

Reluctantly, I promised.

The next night at dinner, I told Daddy everything except the scary parts. I told him about the flyers, my speeches, and Principal Griggs's disapproval. To my relief, he chuckled. "Whose idea was it to make the flyers hot pink?" he asked.

Zach slammed down his fork, nearly upsetting his water glass. "Let me get this straight. She gets called into the principal's office, and you think it's funny?"

Daddy looked surprised. "Nothing really bad happened."

"The last time I had to go see the principal, you grounded me for three weeks."

"There's nothing funny about being an underachiever, Zach. This was just a prank."

I winced. *Underachiever* was undoubtedly Zach's least favorite word. It had hounded him most of his life, in spite of the fact that when it came to pure smarts, he was probably my superior. He always beat me in Monopoly and chess, and his knowledge of history, math, and geography far surpassed my own. It was strange to me that he knew so much but never seized the opportunity to shine. Maybe he needed his own Black Beast to goad him to success. Whatever the reasons for his reticence, I knew that we were on dangerous footing. Zach didn't like to be compared to me.

"We'll just see what's funny," he muttered under his breath. I searched his face for clues as to what he was planning, but it was distorted by his vigorous chewing—big, meaty mouthfuls, ground to a pulp. It didn't bode well. I should have found some way to placate him: offer to do the dishes for a week, clean his room, shine his shoes, something. I knew it at the time, but I let the moment pass, too pleased that I hadn't upset my father.

The next day was a Saturday. I usually tried to sleep in, to make up for all the sleep I had lost during the week working on "the project" with Daddy. But I was rudely awakened early that morning by my mother ripping the comforter off my bed. "Get up and come in the den," she said. It was her martinet voice, to be obeyed at once.

I wrapped my robe around me, shivering. I had a presentiment of what was coming, but when I went in the den, the reality was worse than I had anticipated. Daddy was scrunched in the corner of the couch, puffing on a Salem as if it was his last cigarette before execution. And so it was. All the drawers to his desk were pulled wide open, and the blueprints we'd been working on were strewn across the room. I hadn't realized there were so many.

"What's all this?" my mother demanded.

"Looks like blueprints to me," I said.

"Don't you get smart with me. I mean, what have you two been up to behind my back?"

I looked at Daddy. Please don't tell her the truth, I silently pleaded. Please let us keep our nights together; they're all I've got. For a moment, he returned my gaze, and there was sadness in his eyes. And something more I hoped I'd never see: defeat, and a consciousness of betrayal. He shrugged and looked away. "Terri Lynn's been helping me draw up plans for the Volkshouse."

"And when has she been doing this?"

"After school," he said, which was a lie and wasn't.

"That's not what I hear. I hear you've been keeping her up until all hours of the morning."

"I wouldn't say all hours—"

"And what do you think you're doing, working on this in the

first place? You promised me, no more big dreams. You promised me, Jack. A quiet life. You promised." Her voice got quavery, and for a moment, I thought she might be about to cry. But her fury won over, and she started rolling up all the blueprints, without any regard for the delicacy of the paper. "I'm putting these in my closet," she said. "And that's where they're going to stay, at least until we get back on our feet."

I waited for Daddy to protest. He said nothing, just kept looking into the distance and puffing away. The slump of his shoulders terrified me. I went over and sat down close to him, laying my head on his chest. "Blow me a smoke ring, Daddy," I said. I wanted something familiar, however evanescent, to fill up the awful silence my mother had left in her wake. He blew a couple of practice rings, then one magnificent oval that hung in the air like a melody and gradually disappeared. We watched as it evaporated, bit by bit, leaving nothing behind but a memory of transient perfection. He stubbed out his cigarette carefully— once, twice, and on the third twist of his wrist, he stood up and headed toward the door.

Panicked, I grabbed his arm and said, "There will be others, you know." I didn't have to explain what I meant—other perfect smoke rings, other plans, other chances for glory. He knew, and it didn't matter. He shook his head, hugged me tightly, and said, "I've got to get out of here, baby." The next sound I heard was the one that I had dreaded all my life: the front door closing behind him.

Maybe if I hadn't been possessed by a Beast, my whole life would have gone differently then. Maybe I would've gone back to bed and cried myself to sleep. Maybe I would've been sad, or mad, or some other emotion appropriate to the moment. Then finally, having felt enough, the emotion would be over. But the Black Beast didn't operate that way. He feasted on feelings, gobbling them up and swallowing them down in a wild feeding frenzy. I was so overcome by the swirl of emotions coursing through my body, I had to sit down and put my head between my knees. I couldn't breathe. I wanted to die. No, worse—I wanted to kill.

Killing my mother would solve everything. Maybe I'd kill Zach along the way too—he must have been the one to squeal. Zach had long since graduated from cap guns to BBs. I'd seen what he could do to crows: one shot—*bang!*—right between the eyeballs, and they came plummeting down from the telephone wires. Our backyard was littered with dead and dying crows, and sparrows, and pigeons. I'd have to sneak into his room to steal a gun, but I was smart; I knew that I could do it. Maybe I could even somehow make it look like Zach had killed my mother, then turned the gun on himself.

My mother chose that inopportune moment to come back in the den. "Where did your father go?" she asked.

"You drove him away. Are you happy? Are you thrilled? Are you satisfied now?" The words kept pouring out of me, each one faster than the last, until there was nothing left in my mouth but bile and spit. So I spat at her. She raised her hand to slap me, but the Black Beast's reflexes were just as quick.

I honestly don't know who struck the first blow, but within seconds we were scratching, hitting, kicking each other, like a pair of mauling tigers. It felt almost as good as smashing glass. For a moment, my mind slipped sideways and I was that little four-year-old girl again, trapped inside a cage, unable to get free. I grabbed a handful of my mother's hair and yanked with all my might. She screamed with pain and twisted my arm hard behind my back, until I buckled to my knees. She stepped back, and we stared at each other, both of us shocked and panting.

"Just wait until I tell your father."

I wondered about that. "No hitting" was one of his few inexorable rules.

"You hit me first," I said coolly.

"I did not."

"Did so. And it doesn't matter anyway. Who do you think he'll believe?"

We continued to stare into each other's eyes, aware of the enormity of that moment. Blood had been spilled between us at last—literally. There was a long scratch on my forearm from my mother's ring, welling up and soaking into the white plush of my terry-cloth robe.

She didn't have to tell me to go to my room. There was nothing left to say, nowhere else to go. I lay down on my bed, pulling the sheet up over my head and sucking on the scratch. I tried to still my pounding heart, but the Black Beast wasn't satisfied. Blood. He wanted more blood.

"Enough," I tried to argue.

"More."

My heart was beating so hard by then, I was afraid it would burst through my chest. Toto was lying on the pillow next to me, and I reached out and pulled him close. Hugging Toto was usually a surefire soother, but not this time. I'd forgotten about my scratch, and a smear of blood corrupted his pale yellow fur — the fur I'd tried so hard to keep clean. Was there nothing pure left on this earth to comfort me? The world was a foul and filthy mess, and the Black Beast wanted revenge.

I had a good idea what he wanted to do, and it shocked and sickened me. Nausea churned in my stomach, and again I tasted bile. Feeling flushed and hot, I tried to toss off the sheet, but it got tangled up between my legs. By the time I finally kicked myself free, I was all in a sweat. I swung my bare feet off the bed and pressed them hard against the floor, hoping the contact with something solid would somehow reassure me. It didn't. I knew then that the only way I'd feel better was to surrender.

Despite the Black Beast's goading — "Now!" he urged me. "Faster!" — I walked slowly on tiptoe down the hall to my parents' bathroom, careful to avoid the traitorous fifth and seventh floorboards. Silently, I closed the door behind me and eased open the creaky medicine cabinet. I'd grown quite a bit in the last several months and was able to reach the top shelf with no problem. I pulled down my father's straight-edge razor, unscrewed the bottom as I'd watched him do so many times, and slipped out the sharp, shiny blade.

The question was not what to do with it; the question was where on my body to do it. For a fleeting second, I contemplated my wrists. But tendons were tough, I'd learned in school, and besides, I didn't want to die. To exact revenge, I needed to be alive. The problem was, what with my cheerleading outfit and dance leotard, so much of my body was exposed all the time. Where could I safely draw blood?

I slipped off my robe and examined my body, inch by inch. There was really only one secret place left: the thatch of bright red pubic hair that had sprouted this past year. No one ever looked at me there. It was mine to do with as I pleased—the very last comfort zone left.

My hands were shaking as I parted the hair and exposed a naked patch of skin just below my pubic bone: virgin skin, that had never seen sunlight. A drop of sweat ran off my nose and splashed against my inner thigh. I licked my lips and made a tiny incision, no longer than my fingernail. It didn't hurt. On the contrary, when the razor sliced through my skin, followed by a thin rivulet of red, a vast and deep calm settled over me. I could feel my heart begin to slow down, until I could count the separate beats. One, two, three, one, two, three—smooth and steady as a waltz. I made another nick a little farther down, and again the sight of blood pacified me. I felt quiet and dreamy, as if I were about to fall asleep.

The fact that I was injuring my own body didn't really occur to me. That wasn't how it felt. I was my mother's creation, and every cut spited her, not me. Revenge can still be sweet even if it's secret. It didn't matter that she didn't know what I was doing. God knew, and I trusted Him to properly assign the blame.

My father didn't call, and I didn't know where he was. Those were desperate days: endless anxious afternoons and frantic sleepless nights, where I imagined everything that could have happened to him. Cutting myself was the only thing that helped soothe me, and I continued to do so until my pubic area was a mass of tiny nicks. They itched like the devil, and I worried about infection. Normally, I'd ask my mother how I could treat it, but we weren't speaking to each other. Both of us were like live wires, snapping with electricity; contact would have meant an explosion. I knew, although I didn't ask her, that she too was just living for the sound of my father's key in the door—assuming we ever heard it again.

When we finally did, a few days later, I held my breath. I was certain that the first words out of my mother's mouth would not be "Where have you been?" but rather, "Terri Lynn hit me." I waited, nervously watching her lips, ready with my rebuttal. But Daddy passed right by her, giving me a quick kiss on the forehead, on the way to his room. She didn't speak—apparently my father was getting the silent treatment too. I was emboldened by that. I figured my mother must be feeling her share of the guilt, or else she would have told him straight away.

I almost wished she had. Maybe we could have had it out then and there; and even if I was punished, no punishment could have been more severe than the one that ultimately ensued. We didn't stop. The fights between us just got worse— always in private, and escalating in violence. We used every weapon at our disposal: fingernails, fists, sharp-heeled shoes. We fought everywhere, in every room of the house, in the backyard, in the car, whenever and wherever we were alone together. The slightest thing would set us off: a look, a word, the absence of a look or word. It didn't matter. Dry tinder finds a match somehow.

Up until then, with very few exceptions, I had somehow managed to keep my meltdowns from everyone except my mother. None of my teachers could have suspected what I was really like, and certainly none of my friends, because they never saw me out of control. Zach knew what I was capable of, but even he never witnessed the madness between me and my mother.

It was a monstrous secret that grew harder and harder to keep hidden as the bruises began to appear. "What happened to your leg?" my father would ask. "I blew a pirouette," I'd quickly explain, or something in that vein. Once, only once, a teacher asked me about a mark on my neck. It was my favorite teacher, Mrs. Gayle, and I couldn't tell if she was truly concerned or just making conversation. I shrugged. "Redheads bruise easily," I said. This soon became my mantra with the girls on the cheer-leading squad too. "Redheads bruise easily." Indeed they do.

To my surprise, my mother lied even more smoothly than I did. "Julia, how'd you get that scratch on your cheek?" my father asked one night. "I was petting the neighbor's cat," she said without a moment's hesitation. Nothing in her eyes changed. Her beauty stayed intact—a useful distraction—although I may have been the only one to notice that a few stray lines had started to creep into her brow.

I no longer watched her get dressed for the evening on those rare occasions when she and my father would go out together. For one thing, she didn't invite me into her room anymore.

Somehow she managed to handle all those little hooks and clasps I used to fasten for her. She untangled her pearls by herself. She decided, in her sole and absolute discretion, which shoes went best with which purse. It must have been a very lonesome time for her, getting all dolled up for the night with no one's eager eyes to mirror her.

But if she never asked for my company, I never offered it, either. I didn't want to see her naked. I was too afraid I'd witness the evidence of my uncontrollable temper on her formerly almost perfect skin—almost, but for the scar on her leg from those jealous little girls so long ago, who couldn't bear her beauty. How I'd hated them every time my mother told me that story. I wanted to go back and beat them up, every single last sneering one. I wanted to make it all better for her. But I couldn't, and I never would, because I was the stone-thrower now.

4

Of tangled things and wild things
The mind must choose to dwell upon
Of circles without central points
That never end, round on and on . . .
What hopeless clutter clouds the brain!
What rushing, racing spurs of thought
Obscure the tracks of order's way,
Obscure the circle's centrodot.

—Age sixteen

The nuns had done their best to instill in me

an unwavering belief in miracles: the loaves and the fishes, smooth-skinned lepers, Lazarus, and the like. It's strange that I was always so ready to believe in fairy tales but not in Bible stories. Perhaps because I fancied myself a writer, miracles seemed too neat a trick, like a literary device whipped out for the occasion to make a story pretty.

That all changed by the time I was sixteen.

By then, I had actually seen firsthand that miracles do happen, even to ordinary folk like me. Nineteen seventy-six witnessed the resurrection of my father's dream, the Volkshouse. Although Daddy and I had been forced to stop working on the project, and the blueprints were stashed away in my mother's closet, that hadn't kept him from pitching the idea whenever he could (out of my mother's hearing, naturally) to anyone who would listen. And damn if he didn't find the money. He and a few risk-seeking partners convinced the Federal Housing Administration that it would be a grand idea to build several tracts of government-subsidized low-income housing way the hell out past nowhere, in a godforsaken swath of desert poetically named Hesperia.

At that time, there was little more to the township of Hesperia than a truck stop, a general store, and some monstrous tumbleweeds. The first time we took the long drive out there, I actually entertained a treacherous thought. "Who'd ever want to live out here?" I said, regretting the words before they were out of my mouth. But my father didn't take offense. Perhaps because he'd grown up in a similar one-drag town, he knew how to dream through the dust. "You just wait," he said. "In a couple of years, we'll be turning people away."

It took a bit more than a couple of years, but in the end he was right. Volkswagen objected to the term Volkshouse, so the name was changed to Custom Homes, which I always thought was hilarious because there was nothing custom about them: four slabs of stucco, a garage port, and a gravel-strewn driveway. *Finito.* Next house.

Sundays were now spent driving around the desert—my mother still in the back seat, of course—looking for new lots. Since they contained nothing but dirt and the odd yucca tree, they were, appropriately enough, dirt cheap. By the time other builders caught on to the idea that there might be a gold mine out here, my father had already bought up the best of the lots, and construction was well under way.

Money is no panacea, of course, but it's a powerful sedative. With the influx of money, a relative calm descended over our house. Daddy was finally able to quit his indentured servitude at Brew 102. My mother also gave up the night shift for more amenable hours. She was significantly less on edge then, less ready to pounce, and she and my father seemed to reach a truce of sorts. Now they fought only about his alleged infidelities, not so much about money.

To my surprise and relief, the fights between my mother and me also grew fewer. It helped that I was spending every available minute in Hesperia, alone with my father in his tiny office with the red rock roof. It might sound boring, building homes out in the middle of the desert, but it wasn't. It was thrilling, watching the wasted landscape slowly blossom with signs of life, meeting the eager families who couldn't believe they were about to afford their very own homes. "We're not selling houses," my father used to say, "we're selling hope." He took me out to all the construction sites, regaling the poor, sweaty workers with news of my latest academic achievements. To this day, the smell of sawdust is my Proustian madeleine: it brings back a life.

Everything was going so well at last. For my sixteenth birthday, over my mother's strenuous objections, my father gave me a 1965 Corvette convertible—white, with a red interior and the original black-and-yellow California license plates. It was, in car lovers' parlance, "cherry." I was elected to the Student Council that year, for the umpteenth time in a row. I was also president of our cliquish YWCA club, the Mauna Loas. (Only popular girls need apply.) And I found a mentor in my beloved English teacher Miss Miller, who recognized my mind's need to run free and excused me from classes to write and read whatever I liked.

It would have been a happy, even ecstatic time, but for one thing: the sudden and unexpected betrayal of my body. I'd gone through puberty smoothly enough a few years before, with all the usual bumps and grinds: the terror of my first menstruation, the strange swellings and sproutings here and there. Somehow I'd managed to stay connected to my body throughout that rite of passage. But at sixteen, the moorings came loose. My body was no longer the container for my soul. It was an enemy, out to shame and humiliate me at every opportunity.

All these years later, I still don't find it easy to write about my archnemesis, my scourge, the bane of my existence: acne. I realize that may sound anticlimactic. All teenagers get acne. It's just a passing phase, a hex of the hormones.

Maybe for somebody else.

A pimple was not just a pimple to me. It was tangible impurity, and it didn't matter to me that everyone else was fighting it too. I'd never been like everyone else. I'd spent my entire life trying to avoid the appearance of imperfection. Nothing was scarier to me than a visible flaw, except perhaps my father's leaving; and in fact, the two were inextricably linked in my mind. Show a flaw, lose a father.

No doubt my perception was distorted. I didn't even have that bad a case, objectively; at most, I probably got one or two new pimples a week. But perhaps—just perhaps—there was some undercurrent of truth to my fear about my father, because he was uncharacteristically critical about my acne. I'll never forget the morning I woke up with a huge, glaring pimple right in the center of my forehead. I tried makeup, which only made it look worse. I tried squeezing it, but it wasn't ready, and I ended up with an angry red swelling the size of a dime. Finally, in desperation, I pulled on an old Dodgers baseball cap and went in to breakfast. Girls didn't wear baseball caps to school in those days, at least not to my school, and it looked decidedly odd with the rest of my outfit. (I had a Student Council meeting that day and was wearing my best three-piece suit.)

My father took one look at me and asked, "What's with the hat?"

"It's the latest thing," I lied. "Casual conservative."

"Well, it looks ridiculous. Take it off."

"Everybody's doing it."

"And if everybody else was smoking pot, does that mean you would too?"

As a matter of fact, everyone else *was* smoking pot, but thus far I'd abstained out of respect for my parents' wishes and fear of damaging the only part of me I still rather liked about myself: my agile brain.

"No, of course not," I said.

"Then take it off."

Reluctantly, I pulled the cap off my head and revealed the pimple, which was no doubt even more swollen now than when I'd last looked in the mirror. My father stared at me, and when he spoke, after what seemed like ten minutes, he sounded shocked.

"Baby, you've got a pimple on your forehead."

"I know." I burst into tears.

"How long do you think it will take that thing to go away?"

"Four, maybe five days."

"Well, you certainly can't go to school looking like that." He picked up the phone and got me excused from classes for the rest of the week. I believed in my heart he was only trying to protect me—kids can be so cruel, and I was such a sensitive girl—but his reaction only reinforced my belief that the world was not a safe place to show one's scars.

I was missing an awful lot of school—my father never hesitated to excuse me when he felt my pimples demanded it—until a complication arose. Tryouts were being held for junior varsity cheerleader. I'd always been a cheerleader, from grade school on. I couldn't imagine not being one. Cheerleading was part of my identity; it was who I saw in the mirror. And ironically, all the attention that came along with it kept people from looking too close: all they saw was the cute little uniform. I felt safe inside the stereotype.

But tryouts meant I'd have to go to school every single day for the next three weeks to learn the routines and campaign for votes. How could I possibly do that when I couldn't predict from one morning to the next what my external appearance would be? Courtesy of the Black Beast, I already didn't know how I'd feel from day to day. Now I didn't know how I would look. My world was a giant pendulum that someone else was swinging. Neither my body nor my mind really belonged to me or felt within my control.

The solution finally struck me when I was watching my father shave one morning. He nicked himself, and neither of us thought twice about it when he went out of the house with a Band-Aid still attached to his skin. I realized then that the pimples themselves weren't actually the problem. It was the label affixed to them: "acne vulgaris," our family doctor had said. (There were, perhaps, uglier words in the universe, but if there were, I couldn't imagine them.) No one would harbor the same disgust if the pimples were something else—an innocent wound of some kind, for example.

That was one of my first recognitions of the all-important power of the label. Call something one thing, and you'll evoke a shudder. Call it something else, and nobody will care. It was a marvelous way of wielding power, a discovery I would never forget. (Years later, I was asked on certain nasty forms if I'd ever been diagnosed with a psychiatric illness. "Hypothalamic disorder," I answered, which was just another fancy way of saying "depression." It never raised an eyebrow.)

So that morning, once again I picked up Daddy's razor. I had stopped cutting myself between my legs when the fights between my mother and me had deescalated. But I hadn't forgotten the feeling of serenity the nicks of the razor had delivered. Holding my breath and steadying my hand against the mirror, I put the tip of the blade against the rawest, reddest pimple, and cut a quick X through the center. Blood and a thick white fluid oozed out and trickled down my face. It was deeply disgusting, and even more deeply soothing. The pimple no longer looked like a pimple anymore. It looked like I'd been in some kind of accident. I quickly put a Band-Aid over it and went out to face the day.

It worked. I got a few questions, of the "What happened to you?" variety, but I remembered my mother's old explanation for the cuts I'd once made on her face with my fingernails. "A neighbor's cat scratched me," I said. That same neighbor's cat scratched me several more times over the next three weeks, but all it yielded were a few jokes and some ribbing. I suppose it would have been enough just to cover the pimples without cutting them first, but for some reason that felt like a lie. Plus I was afraid the Band-Aids might fall off during cheerleading practice, and then my lie would be exposed. So I just kept on cutting and cutting, each time experiencing a wave of solemn satisfaction that I was outsmarting the world.

I couldn't outsmart my mother, though. "What cat?" she asked me suspiciously when I tried to explain my Band-Aids at dinner. Fortunately, my mother never talked to our neighbors, so she didn't know I was lying when I described the fictitious litter of kittens that had just been born next door. "They pay me two bucks a day for feeding them," I continued, knowing that would make it okay.

She really couldn't blame me, anyway. For as long as I could remember, I'd been taught the essential lesson that the way things looked was far more important than the way things actually were. I never thought to question that lesson—the unshakable foundation of my early life. All I knew of its origin was that it went way back to before I was born, and it had something to do with a baby blue Cadillac.

It seems that when my father was courting my mother, he made up all sorts of stories about his fabulous wealth, when, in fact, he was living out of a suitcase in a Santa Monica flophouse, subsisting on cans of chili and Spam. But Daddy had considerable charm, if nothing else. He looked like a young Frank Sinatra, wavy-haired and slim as the cigarette he held between two fingers, only occasionally bringing it to his lips to take a drag—as if he had a hundred more cigarettes at his disposal and could afford to let this one burn out, or not, at his leisure.

But it took the baby blue Cadillac to convince my mother of his worth. She could choose from plenty of eligible men. She didn't need a mysterious young man whose only stated profession was "sales." My mother hadn't been bred to appreciate mystery. She was from good, solid farm stock, her family's roots planted deep in the earth. They'd made an excellent living out of the cold, hard soil of eastern Canada, enough to send my mother to the best nursing school around, where she was fully expected to catch herself a man. A doctor, they all hoped. Or at the very least, a dentist. With those cheekbones, those hips, that thick mane of hair, how could she possibly fail? But they didn't count on New Year's Eve, and the annual hospital charity ball, or on my father's inexplicable way with women. Somehow he managed to convince my mother to be his date for the gala, despite the fact that she had several other invitations, all of them from interns or residents. "Just you wait," he promised her. "You'll be the queen of the ball."

So she waited and waited, all dressed up in her cinched-waist ball gown with three stiff layers of petticoats scratching her knees. She waited, and she itched. She waited, and she fumed. But at last, an hour late, my father showed up, and the wait was well worth it.

She could hear it coming all the way down the street: a low, throaty purr, like the MGM lion. Then two sudden beeps of the horn, so loud and brash they startled the roosting pigeons out of the tree beneath her window. She stepped out onto the balcony, looked down, and there he was: street light shining on his smooth, wavy hair, right arm draped casually across the wheel of the most beautiful baby blue Cadillac my mother had ever seen.

"It was love at first sight," she told me time and again,

describing that moment. It's a phrase that always puzzled me, because that was not my parents' first date. It was also, naturally, not my father's car. He had sweet-talked the dealer into letting him borrow it for that night only. So, the truth: my mother fell in love with a baby blue Cadillac. Under the spell of the infatuation, she accepted my father's proposal that very night. The next morning, of course, he had to return the car.

I heard this story often and early enough to absorb the message: appearances were extremely important in our family. And if you had to lie to uphold them, so be it.

Maybe it was the weird bandages on my face, or maybe it was just my time for the world to fall apart. Whatever the reason, I didn't make junior varsity cheerleader. I lost. Let me repeat: I lost. Losing out on junior varsity cheerleader may not sound like much of a catastrophe, but for me it felt cataclysmic. When you're chemically unstable, even the most insignificant thing can kick off a major episode of mania or depression.

I'd never lost anything before in my life. Okay, maybe the odd game of Monopoly or chess with Zach, but never anything that really mattered to me. I always got incredibly nervous before elections or exams, but I always aced them. Always. That was just the way my life worked. Panic and succeed, panic and succeed.

I literally couldn't imagine life outside the pantheon. How would I ever face my friends? My enemies? The teachers? The neighbors? The mailman? The guy who cleaned the pool? My mind reeled, and the list went on and on.

When I got the call telling me I hadn't made the squad,
I handled it like a lady. "Thank you," I said politely. Then I
reached down and yanked the telephone cord out of the wall.
I couldn't bear the thought of the inevitable calls: "Did you
make it? Did you make it?" What could I possibly say? I tried to
pronounce the words "I lost," but they wouldn't come out of my
throat. I had to struggle to breathe, as if I were having an asthma
attack.

My parents were in the kitchen. They'd been eagerly await-
ing that phone call too. My mother had even made cupcakes
with orange and black icing, the school colors. "Congratulat—"
they started to shout. Then they saw the stricken look on my
face, and the shout died on their lips.

"What's wrong, baby? Was there a tie?" my father asked.

I shook my head, still speechless.

"You can't mean—"

I nodded.

"No."

I nodded again.

"Well, what do you know about that," he said and sank back
into his chair.

My mother tried to soften the blow. "There's always next year,"
she said. "Varsity cheerleader's much better than junior varsity."

It's easy to look back on your life and see the moments that
might have changed everything if they were handled differently.
I've often wondered if my father had taken me into his arms, or
if my mother had said, "Don't worry, sweetie. We love you anyway," what my life might have been like after that. I didn't need

to be taught how to win, but I desperately needed to know how to lose. I never learned that lesson.

An awkward silence stretched out between us. We were in foreign territory, and nobody knew what to say. Finally, I said, "I'm exhausted. I'm going to my room." And so I did. For twenty-one days.

It was the longest continuous period of despondency I'd ever experienced. I didn't want to watch TV. I didn't want to read. I could barely be bothered to breathe: what was the point of sucking air out of a universe that so clearly despised me? I didn't even come out for meals, although a gnawing, unappeasable hunger tormented me. I stayed in my room until everyone else was asleep, then I crept to the kitchen and devoured everything in sight: the leftovers from dinner, giant bowls of cereal, all the cookies in the cookie jar, slices of bread slathered with butter, heaping tablespoons of brown sugar, chocolate syrup straight out of the can. I consumed anything that didn't need defrosting—even odd things, like iced coffee packets and raw pancake mix. It didn't matter what I ate, it wasn't enough to fill up the sinkhole in my heart, the big caved-in place where my confidence and self-esteem used to be.

My mother noticed the missing food, and at first she accused Zach, whose appetite was indeed enormous. When Zach denied it, she turned to me. "I can't help it," I said and started to cry. "I'm starving." My mother never could stand the sight of my tears, and that was the last she said about it. I think it was easier for her to just replace the food than try to reason with my inexplicable hunger.

To stay out of school, at first I faked a tummy ache. Then the flu. Then asthma. Then the flu again. But by the end of ten days, even my father was growing concerned about how much time I was missing, although he dutifully picked up my homework for me. I couldn't do the work, so it didn't much matter, but he insisted.

"Should we send her to the doctor, do you think?" he asked my mother.

"She's just having one of her spells," she replied. "Ignore it, and she'll get bored soon enough."

I was way past bored. Bored would have been a pleasant relief from the intensity of pain I was experiencing. It was physical—so physical I wondered if, indeed, I did have the flu. My joints ached. The knuckles on my fingers throbbed, and the muscles in my face and throat felt so stiff and sore, it was an effort to speak. So I said less and less, just "yes," "no," and "I don't want to." With one exception: my acne got so bad, I finally called the doctor to see what he could do. He prescribed a strong dose of steroids—hardly the best medication for someone with chronic depression, but of course, I didn't know that then. From that point on, I slid into a bottomless, black void, a place so dark and desolate that I was astonished to see the sun rise every morning, as if it were just another cloudless, temperate Southern California day and not the end of all life as I knew it.

In the beginning, my friends called every day to see how I was doing.

"Rhonda's on the phone," my father would say.

"Tell her I'm in the shower."

"Maria wants to talk to you."

"Tell her I'm in the shower."

Allison, Elisa, Patty, Donna, Carrie—practically all the Mauna Loas called. I was always in the shower, until, finally, they gave up.

All except Rhonda. One of the reasons she was my best friend was that she didn't take no for an answer. Whenever I would drop out of sight, which was often, she would pester me until I agreed to see her—although not until the worst of the "spell" had passed. But about a week into my illness, Rhonda also stopped calling. I was filled with foreboding because I knew she wasn't one to give up so easily. Sure enough, the next night, there was a knock at our door. My mother peeked through the kitchen blinds, then came into my bedroom to tell me it was Rhonda. I froze.

"You can't let her see me like this!" I pleaded. I hadn't showered in a week. My hair was lank and stringy; no doubt I even smelled bad. Then came another knock, this one louder than the first. "Just don't answer it," I begged my mother. "She'll go away eventually."

"She saw me peeking through the blinds," my mother said. "I can't pretend I didn't see her."

I thought fast and furiously. "If you let her in, she'll see what a mess the house is in, and she'll tell her mother. You know what a gossip she is; she'll tell everyone. It's obvious we're not fit for company."

That struck home. My parents almost never entertained because, in my mother's opinion, the house was never "fit for company." "Fit for company" was deep, dark code: it meant that everything had to be spotless, shiny, and pristine. As a result, to this day I have an immense fear of guest towels. Whenever those tiny, delicate, intricately embroidered monsters emerged from the linen closet, I knew there was big trouble ahead. Inevitably, they would be followed by a week of dust rags and silver polish, Lysol and Windex, and frozen dinners for breakfast and lunch.

Zach and I learned early on that my mother was not to be disturbed, under any condition, during this sacred cleansing ritual. Sneezes were stifled, coughs suppressed, and heaven help me if my asthma kicked up. Thank God we had house guests only once every five years, if that. I can remember only three occasions, in fact, when we actually had someone to dinner.

Odd, that in a house that so rarely had visitors, we had so many matching sets of guest towels. We also had complete sets of linen tablecloths and napkins, and a rosewood box of "good" silver and china, which we ourselves were apparently not good enough to use.

My mother looked around her. My bedroom was a shambles. There were chocolate syrup stains on my sheets, books strewn all about the floor, and dust bunnies in the corners. The rest of the house wasn't much better. Although she was a stickler for personal hygiene, my mother worked hard at her job, and the housework often suffered as a result. For a moment, I pitied her predicament.

"Can't you just see her out by the pool?" she asked.

"Look at me," I said. I was an even bigger mess than the house.

She sighed. "All right, I'll tell her you're too sick to get out of bed."

"That won't stop her."

"Then I'll tell her you're contagious."

"Better."

That didn't keep Rhonda from calling, of course, but I'd put such a scare into my mother that she made up excuses for me not to come to the phone, even when I hadn't asked her to. I wallowed in absolute isolation, which was just the way I liked it.

I kept a journal at the time, and the entries got shorter and shorter until they were monosyllabic:

"Same."

"Same."

"Same."

On the twenty-first day (I remember because twenty-one was my lucky number), I woke, at last, to a different sky: dark and brooding, with heavy, gray nimbus clouds threatening rain. Finally, I thought, God gets it. He sees me. I felt the stirrings of change inside me—something was going to be different today. I fell back asleep and didn't wake until my mother came into my room early that evening. "We're going to the movies. Are you sure you don't want to come? It's a comedy; it would do you good to laugh a little."

I shook my head, wondering at her impenetrability. Did this look like a face that could laugh? But as I heard the front door close behind them, I started to think. When was the last time I'd even cracked a smile? I was only sixteen years old, and I could barely remember the last time I'd giggled.

It must have been several months back, at a wedding reception for one of my father's partners. Zach and I had each been allowed a glass of champagne—cheap wedding champagne that went straight to my head. Everything made me laugh after that: the bride's froufrou dress, the nervous toasts, the way the groom's mother kept crying even though the ceremony was long over. I went up to her and said, "You don't approve of this much, do you?" She looked shocked—the groom, standing next to her, even more so.

Remembering he was my father's partner, I said, "So how long till we make our first million? I've got tons of things to buy." My father overheard this and signaled my mother to pull me away. She took me into the bathroom and splashed cold water on my face, which only made me giggle all the harder. When I came back out, I danced the cha-cha all by myself, flinging myself around the dance floor and tripping over the bride's long train, tearing it. My parents decided to call it a night.

I was in no mood for the cha-cha now, but still, a drink might not hurt. My father always seemed to feel better after his nightly scotch: looser, livelier, more talkative. I'd be happy if I just managed to coax a smile out of my pale, pinched lips. So I went to the cabinet where my parents kept the liquor. I'd never really looked inside it before. There were so many bottles—a major waste of money, considering that my father really only drank scotch and my mother just had a glass of wine now and then. It was "company liquor" for the company that never came.

I pulled down a bottle of Kahlúa and took a swig. It was yummy, much better than the acidic, fruity champagne I'd had at the wedding. I smacked my lips and had another swig. It went down even easier than the first one had. The bottle was well over three-quarters full, and I kept on drinking until there was only an inch or so left. That looked suspicious, so I polished off the last inch, then went into the backyard and threw the empty bottle over the fence, which abutted the freeway.

There is something even greater than pleasure, and that is the absence of pain. Midway through the bottle, I realized that my body didn't hurt anymore. What's more, I could move. Whatever invisible wall had existed between me and the outside world was gone. I could feel the wind caress my cheek; I could feel my eyelashes flutter. The rain, which had been looming all day, was falling at last in big splashy drops—just a few at first, then more, and more, until my nightgown was soaked through.

I stripped down to my panties and rolled around in the wet, prickly grass. I could feel each blade against my skin. I could count the raindrops as they fell, even though there were hundreds of them coming at me, all at once. I felt dizzy and slightly sick to my stomach, but more powerful than the heavens. I was making it rain, I realized. My wish for change, and mine alone, had brought about this storm.

Over the growling thunder, I heard a sound I hadn't heard in ages: the Black Beast was roaring with laughter.

Hmm, I thought. Alcohol: very interesting.

I recall little else that happened that night, except that I threw up all over my mother's beloved begonias and somehow managed to crawl back into bed, naked and shivering. I woke the next morning expecting to feel lousy, but I didn't. I felt fine—no, better than fine. It was incredible: after so many weeks of not wanting to speak to a soul, I suddenly wanted to talk to the world.

Luckily, it was Saturday, so my friends weren't at school. I got on the phone and called up everybody, even the girls who'd made junior varsity cheerleader.

"It's me," I said. Then a bit impatiently: "Terri. No, I'm much better now, thanks. Just a bad case of asthma. So tell me, where's the action tonight?" Not "And how have you been?" or "What's new with you?" Just where were the parties, who was going, and how did I get there.

I ran roughshod over a dozen or so of my friends and collected several invitations. The hottest party sounded like the one at Bob Greene's house, down on G Street and Benson. His parents were away for the week, and he was a big star on the water polo team. I'd always had a little thing for Bob Greene, ever since my first day at school, when he'd held the gymnasium door open for me. Manners were scarce enough among the boys at Chaffey High. It didn't take much to impress me.

Tonight, I vowed, I'd make him take notice. I called up Rhonda and told her my scheme.

"But he's going out with Elisa," she said. Elisa was a fairly close friend of mine, a fellow member of the Mauna Loas, to whom I'd pledged eternal sorority.

"How long has that been going on?"

"A week or so."

"Then it's really not etched in blood, is it?"

"Terri, that's not very nice."

"I'm sick and tired of being nice," I said, an edge creeping into my voice. "Nice hasn't gotten me very far with boys, now has it?"

Rhonda knew what I meant. Nobody asked me out. I've spent years trying to figure out why. On paper, I was popular enough. At the very least, people seemed to like me well enough to elect me to the coveted Student Council year after year. I always had someone to sit with at lunch, someone to walk with to classes, someone to talk with during breaks. At my school, the cool kids lounged on the auditorium steps by the statue of the tiger, the Chaffey High mascot. The unfortunates—the fatties, the nerds, the social misfits—were relegated to the plaza by the bathrooms, where there was little shade and the occasional noxious smell. I always hung out by the tiger.

My mother said the boys were intimidated: by my car, perhaps, or all the attention and awards I got from the teachers. My father said the boys were just plain stupid. A lot of them did, in fact, look stupid, but I wondered if boys had a built-in radar telling them which girls would be easy to handle and which ones (like me) might be trouble. I never thought to ask my brother's opinion, because I'd never considered him in the social swim. It was as if we went to separate schools; Zach lived light years away from the tiger.

Deep down, I knew the truth, or rather, the several truths: in a town and a time of life that prized conformity, I was too different from the other girls. I didn't meet the established standard of beauty: I wasn't blonde, I didn't have big breasts or golden, suntanned skin. In fact, I was at my most popular at the very beginning of the school year. Everyone wanted to stand next to me, to compare their summer tans with my paper-white skin.

And although I was a good listener, I didn't know how to talk to boys. I watched intently while my girlfriends chatted blithely, easily, lightheartedly about what seemed to me the most inane and innocuous of subjects: "Patty told Donna she saw Carrie with Jeff at the mall." "No! What did Donna say?"

I'd shake my head in wonder. For the most part, these weren't silly girls. On our own, in the dark, sacred truth of slumber parties, we'd talk about substantial things, things that really mattered: love, life, our future dreams and visions for the world. But as soon as a boy showed up on the horizon, all their substance seeped right out of them, and they turned into froth before my eyes.

I didn't know how to do froth, although I desperately wanted to. When I was interested in a boy, I wanted to traffic in secrets: What were his deepest hopes and fears? His most cherished desires? It made perfect sense to me—how else was I supposed to touch his soul if he wouldn't grant me access? But adolescent boys apparently don't like to be pried open like a can of anchovies. They kept their distance from me, and I spent many a frustrated night longing to be braver and more insubstantial.

I showed up at breakfast that morning with a bright, sunny smile on my face. "Well, look who's back from the dead," my father said. Zach looked up suspiciously from his bowl of raisin bran. My mother put her hand on my forehead. "Your eyes look feverish," she said, "but your skin feels cool enough."

"It's amazing," I said. "I feel completely better." I didn't tell them that a bottle of Kahlúa had been the magic cure. "In fact, I feel so good, I'm ready to tackle my homework now." I took a quick breath, then rushed on. "And there's a party tonight at Bob Greene's—"

"Oh no," my mother said. "If you think you're going out tonight after missing three weeks of school, you've got another think coming."

"But you don't understand. Bob Greene's the most popular boy in school—"

"Never heard of him," Zach mumbled through his cereal.

"—and he invited me especially, Rhonda said. I'm pretty sure he wants to ask me out."

My little white lie was a subliminal ploy. I suspected my parents were actually quite worried about my unusual lack of attention from the opposite sex. And sure enough, my father's eyes flickered over to my mother's. For a moment, their eyes locked; then she gave a brief, almost imperceptible nod.

"If you can finish half your homework by tonight, we'll let you go," my father said. "But only for a couple of hours, and we expect you home by ten."

I jumped up and kissed him, then for good measure, kissed my mother too. I would've kissed Zach, I was so happy, but he scowled and made a cross out of his fingers in the universal "Be-gone, vampire!" language, so I left him alone.

Surrounded by a pile of encyclopedias, I attacked my home-work. I was afraid that after so many weeks of sloth, my brain would be rusty, but it wasn't. It was as if I had an entirely new set of synapses, refurbished and raring to go. The answers came quite easily to me—almost too easily, in fact. The right words were just dancing in the air above my head, and I simply had to snatch them down and let them flow through my pen. And once they started flowing, I couldn't stop them; the only problem was writing them down fast enough.

My geography teacher had asked for a couple of paragraphs on the culture of Tasmania. I gave her six pages, single spaced. Miss Miller wanted a book report on *Macbeth*. Thank God I'd already read that with Professor Tremaine, so it was a breeze. I threw in a totally gratuitous addendum on the possible applica-bility of Freud's dream theory to the sleepwalking scene. Even math, which was usually so hard for me, didn't slow me down. Numbers flashed in front of my eyes like neon signs, shouting "Pick me! Pick me!" and I just had to transcribe them.

I didn't take a break until nearly seven that evening, and by then I was well over halfway through. My parents were watching TV in the den, so I slipped into the kitchen and took a few quick hits of something called Tia Maria. It didn't taste as good as the Kahlúa, but it had the same desired effect: within minutes, I felt as far from scholarly and as close to silly as I could possibly get. I felt—dare I say it?—quite insubstantial.

I got dressed in a hurry, taking care to brush my teeth well to hide the smell of the liquor. I popped my head in the den to say good-bye to my parents. "You're wearing that?" my mother asked, pointing to my skimpy denim miniskirt and slightly-too-tight emerald top, which brought out the green in my hazel eyes. I smiled, knowing that her disapproval must mean I looked a bit sexy. Good. I usually tried to dress nicely for parties, and nicely was obviously getting me nowhere. It was time for a little startle of skin.

Everyone was there: all the junior varsity cheerleaders, of course, and even a smattering of the varsity cheerleaders, which made it the place to be. For a few brief glorious moments, I was the absolute center of attention because nobody had seen me in such a long time. I even saw Bob Greene looking my way, checking me out, and that was all the encouragement I needed. Well, that and a couple of big plastic cups full of beer. Up until then, I'd always avoided drinking at parties, afraid that I would lose control. (The Black Beast was hard enough to handle sober.) Besides, I hated the smell and taste of the warm keg beer that was always served at these large bashes. But now that I knew the Black Beast's affinity for alcohol, I harbored no more fears. I chugged down another cup, chewed some toothpaste, and marched straight over to Bob.

"I'm Terri," I said, interrupting his conversation with another girl. I stuck out my hand. "You held the gym door open for me last year."

He looked a little nonplussed but shook my hand. "Bob

Greene," he said. As if I didn't know. As if his pellucid blue eyes and tousled blond hair, slightly bleached from all the chlorine in the pool, weren't pure slumber party fodder.

Over Bob's shoulder, I saw Elisa look our way and start to head over. There was no time left for subtleties, which was good, because I didn't feel like I had a subtle bone in my body. I hauled out the big guns.

"Do you want to come see my car?" I asked Bob.

"What have you got?"

"A '65 'Vette."

"Oh, so you're the one. Is it true you get a parking ticket every day?"

It was true. My father insisted that I park in the teacher's parking lot because the car would probably be safer there. It meant a ten-dollar ticket every day, but he preferred that to the inevitable dings or worse I would have risked if I'd parked with the other students.

"It's totally worth it," I said. "You'll see." Elisa was almost at his elbow now. "Come on, it's parked just up the street."

Elisa sidled up and put her arm around Bob's waist. "Terri, it's so good to see you back. We were all getting so worried."

"Why, where have you been?" Bob asked.

"Just a slight touch of pneumonia," I said. Then I looked him square in those beautiful eyes. "But I'm feeling much, much better now. Ready for anything." I smiled with all the wattage I could muster. He smiled back.

"Elisa, would you mind getting me another beer? This one's warm," he said.

"They're all warm," Elisa said, eyeing me suspiciously.

"There's some cold Buds in the refrigerator. And while you're at it, could you make me a sandwich too? Mom left some cold cuts and stuff in the crisper."

"Are you kidding? The swim team's been in the kitchen for the last half hour, getting stoned. I'm sure they've eaten everything that doesn't move by now." Elisa clearly refused to budge, and Bob finally stopped trying to get her to.

"Well, I'm gonna go check out Terri's car. I'll just be a couple of minutes."

"Ooh, I'd love to go for a ride in the 'Vette," Elisa said.

I admired her stubbornness, but not enough to invite her along. "Sorry, it's a two-seater," I said. "But definitely some other time." I turned my back so as not to see her expression.

The car was actually parked several blocks away, which gave Bob and me a little more time to get to know each other—or rather, gave me more time to talk. I wanted to know everything, all at once: Who were his heroes? Did he believe in life after death? Was it hard to think underwater? I was so excited and nervous, the words just tumbled out of my mouth. I could feel my lips moving way too fast, like I was munching popcorn during a scary movie. It was difficult speaking slowly enough to be understood, and even more difficult waiting for Bob's replies. But once we got to the 'Vette, it spoke for itself.

Ah, the lovely lines of that car. It looked like it was moving even when it was standing still. Bob gave a long wolf whistle. "Wow!" he said. "It's gorgeous."

"It's fuel-injected," I said proudly, not quite sure what this meant. "Come on, get in."

I put the top down, and we sat side by side, just the chrome stick shift between us. I turned on the radio—Art Garfunkel was warbling "Bridge over Troubled Water." It was a delicious moment: me and Bob and the 'Vette and the stars, with only the man in the moon as our witness.

Bob turned to me. "Is it a standard H-shift?" he asked.

Oh, fuck the car, I wanted to say. But I nodded. "Here, I'll show you." I reached over and took his hand and placed it on the stick shift. Then I switched on the engine, and that inimitable growl filled the evening air, drowning out Art Garfunkel. As it settled into a sexy rumble, I put my hand on top of Bob's and guided him through the motions of shifting.

"It's a really short bridge," he said. Again, not quite sure what this meant, I nodded and said, "It's the best."

For the first time since we'd got in the car, Bob looked at me directly. "You know, you've got really pretty hair," he said. He reached out and brushed it back from my face. "Soft, too."

I flushed, not with embarrassment but with victory. The Black Beast urged me to lean over and plant a big kiss on Bob's lips, and it took all the self-control I could muster to keep my body still. Boys liked to pursue and conquer, I knew. But I also knew that at this rate, I'd never be kissed. I'd die an old maid, like my great-aunt Bessie, all covered in afghans and cat hair and Liberty prints.

"But what about Elisa?" I suddenly thought.

"To hell with Elisa," the Black Beast hissed. "She just made junior varsity cheerleader. She doesn't need Bob Greene to make her popular. Whereas you, on the other hand . . ."

The Beast was right. Besides, there was no loyalty left in my body, only nerve endings. When Bob's fingers gently touched my cheek, time turned a somersault. On the one hand, it took an eternity for Art Garfunkel to sing the last note. On the other, my heart was beating faster than a dragonfly's wings, and I hovered over the moment, drinking it all in: the night, Bob's touch, the delicate vibrations of the engine. I looked around quickly, to make sure no one was listening. Then I whispered, "If you're nice to me, maybe I'll let you take it for a spin someday."

He whispered back, "How's Friday night? My parents are gone until Saturday, so we can just hang out at my house. I can barbecue, if you'd like."

A date! An actual date! The Black Beast was so exhilarated, I couldn't hold him back. I leaned over boldly in Bob's direction, and finally, his lips met mine: my first authentic French kiss. For an instant, the image of Elisa's face flashed through my mind, but it was quickly flooded by a sea of sensory input. Bob's lips melted into my own. His tongue was in my mouth, warm and probing, and I wasn't quite sure what to do. But he was gentle, if insistent, and my body got the hang of it long before my mind knew how to respond. I put my hand against the nape of his neck and pulled him closer to me.

We'd rounded second base before I finally pulled away—not out of any sense of modesty or discretion but because a police car pulled up alongside us and flashed its lights. "Take it inside," the officer said. I was annoyed by the interruption and was about to say something acerbic back, when Bob put his hand on mine. "I think we'd better go back to the party," he said. "They'll be wondering what happened to us."

"They," of course, meant Elisa, and I was crushed that Bob would still care. A bit huffily, I said, "Maybe I should just go home," and to my surprise, Bob said, "Yeah, maybe that would be best. But I'll see you Friday night. Seven sharp." He kissed me quickly on the cheek and said, "But for now, it's just our secret, right?" And he left.

As I drove home—taking all the side streets, hyperconscious of that cop car patrolling nearby—I pondered the subtext of Bob's words. Maybe he wanted to keep our date a secret until he could tell Elisa that they were through. That would be the gentlemanly thing to do, and it was clear that Bob was a gentleman. (I would probably have let him get to third base, but he didn't press his advantage.) Maybe he wanted to start our relationship fresh, without any encumbrances hanging over it. Yeah, that must be it. For all of a block, I basked in this thought, until I heard the Black Beast snicker.

"You're such a child," he said.

"You call what I was doing just now childish? Hardly," I replied.

"He wants to keep it a secret because you're the other woman."

I was so disturbed by this I almost ran a stop sign. "You're wrong," I said. "Bob really likes me."

"Sure, he likes you when you're like this."

I knew what the Black Beast meant. Had Bob seen me this

same time last Saturday night, in rumpled old syrup-stained pajamas, stuffing my face with raw pancake mix . . .

"And the only reason that you like him is because he's Elisa's boyfriend. Forbidden fruit is always sweeter to you."

I suddenly felt stone-cold sober. It sounded harsh, but it was true. I'd liked the maneuverings, the danger of being caught, the illicit thrill of our encounter, even better than I'd liked being kissed. Who was Bob Greene to me, anyway? A total stranger who knew nothing about my life. Whereas secrecy and I were old flames.

"Don't worry," the Black Beast said in a soothing, conciliatory tone. "You'll make an excellent other woman."

I'm glad that at sixteen I didn't know how true this statement would prove to be. All I knew at that moment was that my first real kiss had been stolen, and I adored the taste of theft.

Big events sometimes turn on little things: my mother had a bad case of the sniffles. Which meant that she didn't go in to work; which meant that she was home all week, watching TV in the kitchen; which meant that I couldn't access the liquor cabinet. Without the elixir of alcohol to fuel his exhilaration, the Black Beast quickly settled back into the doldrums. They weren't quite as bad as the twenty-one days of hell from which I had just emerged, but still I felt (and no doubt looked) quite awful, so I avoided Bob on campus. Miss Miller let me stay in her classroom to read during lunch, and I spent breaks holed up in the girls' bathroom.

Once again, the days turned long and dull, and I grew weary of life. It was all I could do just to get up, get dressed, and drive myself to school. By Friday night—date night—I was a wreck. I needed to be witty, pretty, and sexy, but all I could think of was how empty and meaningless the universe was, how leaden the air felt against my skin. Panicked, I called up Rhonda.

"I can't go," I said as soon as she answered the phone.

"You have to. It's Bob Greene, for Christ's sake."

"I know, I know. Quit pressuring me."

"What did you finally decide to wear?"

I surveyed the contents of my closet, which were strewn about the room. "Nothing."

"That'll make an impression."

"I'm serious. Nothing I own looks good on me." The truth was, nothing fit. I'd been doing my usual late-night eating all week, and I must have gained at least five pounds.

"Then you'd better go with something black. Black is always sexy."

Except when your skin was as sickly pale as a sliver of new moon. But Rhonda was right: when in doubt, grab black.

"Whatever you do, you'd better hurry," she said. "It's already six thirty-five. Aren't you supposed to be there by seven?"

"Oh shit. I've got to go." I hung up and faced myself in the mirror, hands on my hips like a gunslinger getting ready to draw. No doubt about it: that perky, flushed girl that Bob had kissed only a week ago was nowhere to be seen. In her place was a blob of blue-white flesh with a slash of crimson lips. My mother had lent me her lipstick for the evening. What bloomed like cherries against her tanned skin looked like vampire's blood on me.

My body felt heavy and so, so slow. I pulled on a pair of black drawstring pants and a thick black turtleneck sweater. I looked, from various angles, like a beatnik, a ninja, or a refugee from the Vietcong. But it would have to do. I couldn't muster the energy to try on another blessed thing.

I dreaded the moment when Bob answered his door, but he was well-behaved. There was just the slightest pause between beats when he said, "You look . . . great." He leaned down to kiss me on the lips, but I was in no mood to be touched. I turned my head at the very last moment, so his lips just grazed my ear. He led me into the living room (lavish with chintz; I couldn't stand chintz), and I slumped down on the overstuffed sofa.

"So how was your week? Haven't seen you around," he said, sitting down next to me. Close. Too close. I inched away.

"So-so," I said.

"Did anything good happen?"

"No."

"Did anything bad happen?"

"No."

We sat there in awkward silence, the space between us quivering with question marks.

"You seem a little, um, different tonight," he finally said. "Is everything okay?"

I felt my armpits begin to sweat, but I didn't know what to say. I just nodded.

"I guess I should go out and check on the steaks," Bob said, standing up. "How do you like yours cooked?"

For the life of me, I couldn't answer him. Rare, medium, well-done—what difference did it make? The meat was dead and getting deader by the second. I felt like I was going to cry. I shook my head. "I don't care."

"Can I get you a glass of wine while we wait?"

Now *that* the Black Beast could answer. "Yes, please," I said, sitting up slightly straighter.

Bob opened a bottle of Cabernet, poured me a big, full glass of it, and went outside to the barbecue. While he was gone, I took several serious slugs straight from the bottle. I didn't particularly like the taste, but I loved how it felt going down my throat: warm, with a prickly tingle that made me (or at least, my esophagus) feel like I was alive again. I heard Bob slide the screen door open, and I took another quick swig. I barely managed to swallow it before he came back into the room.

"You haven't touched your wine," he said, gesturing to my glass. "Don't you like it?"

"It's fine." I knew that a lady should only sip wine, but for once, I cared more about the way I felt than the way I must have looked. I took a long drink, then a second, then a third, almost emptying the glass. The Black Beast was starting to wake up again, to care about his surroundings. I looked around me. "You know, I really hate chintz."

Bob laughed and refilled my glass. "So do I."

I took another deep drink, then another. "This wine is

delicious. At least *you* have good taste, even if your decorator doesn't. Who's responsible for this mess?"

"Well, actually, my mother."

I buried my face in my glass, hoping to hide my embarrassed blush. "Sorry, I didn't mean—"

"No, it's fine. Would you like some more wine?" I'd finished it without thinking.

"Sure, if you don't mind. I guess I was thirstier than I realized."

By now I was starting to feel relaxed—no, better than re-laxed. Revivified. As if someone had injected adrenaline into my corpselike veins. I kicked off my shoes and swung my legs up onto the couch. "So, Bob, what's it like being big man on cam-pus?" I asked.

He looked a little startled, then sat down next to me. "I don't think I'm all that popular."

"Are you kidding? All the girls want to go out with you. You've got them on a string. They're like yo-yos." I liked the sound of that and repeated it. "Yeah, girls are just like yo-yos to you."

"Really?" He seemed pleased and put his hand on my knee. "I doubt that that's the truth, and besides, I'm not really inter-ested in what all the girls feel. Only one girl at the moment." He leaned in to kiss me, but I wasn't through talking.

"I personally think popularity's way overrated," I said. "I mean, you get to hang out by the tiger. So what? You have to dress like everyone else, talk like everyone else, pretend to care that you're really interested in what they all are saying, when it's usually just trivial bullshit. You know what I mean?"

"But you're a Mauna Loa, aren't you?"

"So?" I took another drink.

"So you're one of them. The popular girls."

"I know. I think it's a drag."

"Then why don't you quit?"

"Are you kidding? And not be popular?"

"But you just said—"

"Yeah, well, I wouldn't listen to me. Let's talk about you. What do you really think about me?" I started to laugh, and couldn't stop.

Bob looked a little nervous. "I think you're smart, and you're pretty, and—you're out of wine. There's another bottle in the fridge; just give me a minute." He came back with a bottle of Chardonnay. "Sorry, no more red. Is white okay?"

"A-Okay." As I watched him pour the wine into my glass, a sudden overwhelming feeling of sorrow came over me. Tears welled up in my eyes. "Just think of all the poor little grapes that gave their lives for this one bottle of wine. I think everything has feelings, don't you? Even this dumb old chintz sofa. Who knows, maybe it hurts when we sit on it." I stood up, felt a rush of dizziness, and sat back down. "Then again, maybe it's just too stupid to notice."

"Well, I'm not too stupid to notice you," Bob said and gave the kiss another try.

"That was a really clumsy transition," I said. "Not worthy of your reputation. If you want to kiss me, just say so."

"Okay, I want to kiss you."

"Why?"

"Because you're smart, and you're pretty, and—"

"You already said that." I felt a drop of sweat trickle down the back of my neck, and I realized I was angry. "I'll bet you give Elisa better reasons than that."

He pulled back. "Let's leave Elisa out of this." He put the cork back into the bottle. "Maybe this wasn't such a good—"

I grabbed him and kissed his mouth so hard that our front teeth clinked together. I pressed my body so tightly against his, I could feel his shirt buttons burning into my breasts, branding the tender skin. He moaned, and for a second I was ten years old again and back in Dan O'Leary's bathroom. Now, as then, the sound frightened me. To my surprise, the Black Beast stepped in to rescue me. It was his game now.

In a sudden veer of mood, I pulled my tongue and body out of Bob's grasp, and held him out at arm's length.

"What's wrong—" he started to say, but I gently placed my forefinger on his lips. I'd read my share of romance novels, so I knew just what to try. I leaned in, until my mouth was nuzzled up against his ear.

"Slowly," I murmured. "Like this."

Then I delicately traced his earlobe with my tongue. Softly, like powder from a courtesan's brush, I fell upon his face and neck: dozens of light little kisses barely ruffling the skin, each one building upon the last, until he was shivering with pleasure. As I started to unbutton his shirt—coolly, deliberately, as if each button were the last of its kind—he moaned again, but this time his moan didn't frighten me. We were in control now, the Black Beast and I. Only God can make a man, or so the nuns had told me. But hey, I could make a man moan.

I had absolute power, and all it once it bored me absolutely. I was sick of Bob's buttons. I started to move on to his belt (another moan), but it was stubborn, and I quickly grew tired of tugging at it. I needed another drink, to make my motions more fluid, to dim the awfully bright lights, to get me back in the proper mood. I was suddenly sleepy; so very, very sleepy. I yawned and reached for my glass of wine.

"No, don't stop now," Bob pleaded. "That felt amazing."

I took a deep swallow, but it went down the wrong way, and I choked. "Put your hands up over your head," Bob said, and he started to thump on my back. I continued to sputter, and I could feel my face turning fiery red.

"Try putting your head down between your knees," Bob said.

As long as I was moving slowly, everything had been fine. But all this frantic commotion stirred up something inside me, and that something wasn't good. My mouth turned to acid, my stomach heaved, and without further warning, waves and waves of wine spewed out of me, all over Bob's jeans and his mother's faux Persian rug.

Not surprisingly, that was the end of Bob and me. The only good thing about throwing up was that it got me sober enough to drive home. I poked my head in the den to tell my parents good night.

"How did it go?" my mother asked.

"Great. I just want to savor the moment, okay?" I slid the doors shut before they could see—or smell—me more closely.

The next day, Saturday, was laundry day. My mother and I always split the chore. It was my job to pick out all my father's shirts from the hamper, sniff them for perfume, and check the collars for lipstick. It was never exactly spelled out to me, but ever since I was a little girl, I'd known that the perfume I was sniffing for was not my mother's Arpège, and the lipstick stains were not her signature shade of cherry blossom red.

Searching for evidence of other women didn't seem the slightest bit strange to me then. My mother was convinced that my father was unfaithful, and I naturally assumed from that that everyone cheats. Perhaps it explains why I was so willing to betray poor Elisa. In any event, I never found any proof of my father's infidelity. But it was as much a part of our family mythology as the infamous baby blue Cadillac.

Although I adored my father, I wasn't in the mood that morning to smell his musty old shirts. A bit of nausea still lingered on, and I noticed my eyes wouldn't focus quite right when I tried to examine the collars.

"You didn't smell that one thoroughly. Really bury your nose in it," my mother scolded me, picking up a shirt I had just discarded and putting it back in the "unsniffed" pile.

"So how did it go with Bob Greene last night?" she asked. "And what kind of name is Greene, anyway? Scottish? Irish?"

I knew what she was really asking, and it annoyed the hell out of me, as always. "Don't worry, Mom, he's a WASP."

"I was just asking; you don't have to get all huffy with me. I just want to make sure you're associating with the right sort of people."

We'd had this argument so many times, I knew where it was heading. I was in no condition for a fight of that magnitude. "The right sort of people" meant white, middle class (or, preferably, upper), and American; no deviations whatsoever allowed. No matter how many times I encountered it, my mother's staunch conservatism always came as a shock to me, especially given my father's breezy liberal politics. It was just another conundrum of their coupling that I hoped to sort out one day when I was older, wiser, and more jaded.

"Did he try to kiss you?" she asked.

My mother was as conservative about sex as she was about national origin. In fact, whenever she was forced to say the word *sex* or anything pertaining to it, she put it in verbal quotes and wrinkled her nose. It was an easy decision to lie to her.

"He tried, but I wouldn't let him," I said.

"Good girl. You know that at your age, boys are interested in only one thing."

I couldn't resist one little tweak. "You mean it's different at your ripe old age?"

"No, come to think of it, it's not. Men are men, whenever."

I finished sorting and sniffing the shirts, and went into the den to call Rhonda. I needn't have phoned—she'd already heard all about last night, except for the part where I'd thrown up.

"Well, you're lucky," she said. "Bob is taking a totally different line. He told Frank Hernandez, who told Patty, who told me, that he had a really great time. He said you were 'good.'"

"What do you suppose he meant by that?"

"Terri, you're so naïve. It means that you were good in bed."

I was shocked, angry, and mortified all throughout the rest of our conversation. All throughout the rest of the weekend. All the way up until Monday morning, when I parked the 'Vette in my usual spot in the teachers' parking lot and found Frank Hernandez and Gary Johnston waiting there for me.

Frank Hernandez was the varsity quarterback; Gary Johnston, the star basketball center. Both of them were way out of my league, but there they were: keying the math teacher's Volvo and waiting for me. I'd purposefully dressed prim that day, in a pure-as-the-driven-snow white shirt, a plaid pleated skirt, kneesocks, and penny loafers. It was as close as I could get, I suppose, to my old St. Madeleine's uniform—to those halcyon days when my reputation was still intact.

"Cool car," Gary said, flashing his famous grin. His perfect teeth were so gleaming white against his coal-black skin, his smile couldn't help but dazzle.

"Can we walk you to first period?" Frank Hernandez asked, taking my heavy book bag from me and slinging it effortlessly over his shoulder.

"Sure," I said, a bit nervously. My mother's paranoia still echoed in my ears. What could they possibly want from me?

As we made our way across the quad, it felt like everyone was watching us. I knew at least one person was: Elisa's eyes were fixed on me, and she was muttering something that looked a lot like a voodoo curse. Bob Greene was standing next to her, and we both looked away at once. It unnerved me so much, I had trouble paying attention to what Frank and Gary were saying.

". . . Saturday night," Frank said. "Everyone will be there. So what do you say we come pick you up around eight?"

"Pick me up for what?" I said.

"The Key Club party. I told you, everyone is going."

"Here, write down your number," Gary said, offering me a Magic Marker and his outstretched hand. In front of the eyes of the whole wide world, I scribbled my digits across his palm.

That wasn't the end of it. For the rest of that week, boys kept coming up to me, chatting about nothing while they checked me out. Elisa and her three closest friends refused to have anything to do with me. Someone scrawled "Slut" across my locker, which took an eternity to scrub off. It was the first time there had ever been a schism in the Mauna Loas, and as president of the club, I felt guilty and responsible—but not so bad that a part of me didn't secretly enjoy the attention I was suddenly getting from boys. I knew there would be a payday eventually, but "eventually" sounded a long ways away, and for the moment, it was bliss.

Success with the opposite sex meant far more to me than just turning a few boys' heads; it made a tremendous difference in the way I saw myself. I might not be the prettiest girl on campus, but if boys were making the effort to flirt, it must mean I was pretty enough. "Pretty enough" was a revelation to me, an epiphany, a cosmic shift. All my life I'd hungered for perfection; this wasn't perfection, but it would suffice. At "pretty enough," I could legitimately be a member of all my clubs. I didn't have to constantly worry and wonder why my gorgeous friends had accepted me as one of their own. At "pretty enough," I belonged.

Every night before I went to bed, I got down on my knees

and thanked Frank Hernandez and Gary Johnston for asking me out, whatever their motives might be. So what if they were just after sex; I'd deal with that if and when it came up. Or so I kept telling myself—nervously, no doubt naïvely, but nonetheless with resolution. Just walking into that Key Club party with Gary on one arm and Frank on the other would, I was sure, change my whole life. I couldn't seem to think beyond that.

My only real worry was that I was steadily depleting my parents' liquor supply. I took a big drink when I could every morning before school to satisfy the Black Beast's cravings and give me enough confidence and pizzazz to flirt back with the boys. I still couldn't figure out how to say nothing, so I just said whatever was on the top of my head: "Do you believe in a penumbra of privacy rights?" "Will there ever be an end to apartheid in our lifetime?" "Do you think Patty Hearst deserves leniency?"

It clearly wasn't the kind of conversation the boys were used to hearing, but they just laughed and egged me on. "Come on, brainiac," one of them said. "Tell us the biggest word you know." My favorite word at the time was *onomatopoeia*, and the boys got a big kick out of the *pee* sound in that.

To solve the liquor dilemma, I decided to shadow Zach one evening. I knew he was drinking too, although not every day, like me. But I could smell it on him when he'd come home late at night. Hanging back a block or so, I followed him to the 7-Eleven over on Mountain and Sixth. He wasn't at all hard to follow. He had a big roaring Pontiac Trans Am by then, and you could hear that engine from miles away.

He got out of his car and walked around the building. Two

minutes later, a scruffy old man emerged from the back and went into the 7-Eleven. He came out carrying two six-packs and a bottle of wine, which he then handed to Zach, who sped away.

Problem solved. I was scared, but not enough to keep me from venturing around the building. Lying there in a little fortress of discarded boxes was a smelly old man, singing something softly to himself. It sounded like "God Bless America."

"Excuse me, sir," I said tentatively. He didn't look up. I spoke more loudly, with all the confidence I could muster. "Excuse me, sir, may I ask you a favor?"

"Who's that? What you want?" the old man said.

I held out a twenty-dollar bill. "I'd like a couple of bottles of wine, please, if you would. Whatever kind you think is the best. And you can keep the change, of course."

I handed the twenty over from as far away as I could manage. The stench of urine was staggering.

He shambled to his feet and took the twenty. He looked me over. "Stinky Pete knows just the thing for a cute little girl like you. You stay right here and watch for pigs."

I watched for pigs, marveling that it was me, Miss Goody Two-Shoes, Miss Straight A's Teacher's Pet, hanging out in a back alley with Stinky Pete. But he delivered. Within a few minutes, he came back with a bagful of liquor. He handed it to me.

"Boone's Farm Strawberry Hill. You gonna love it. All the little girls do."

"Thank you, Mr. Pete," I said.

"Call me Stinky. Everyone do."

Back at home, I opened the bag and pulled out two large

bottles of wine. I couldn't wait to try it, so I barricaded myself in my walk-in closet and took a sip. It was very sweet and not at all hard to swallow, like some of the alcohol in my parents' cabinet had been. It went down just like lemonade, and before I realized it, I had swallowed a third of the bottle. There was no other word for it: I felt mellifluous. "God bless America," I sang softly to myself. "Land that I love . . ."

All the rest of that week, I kept trying to get my parents to go out to the movies and dinner on Saturday night, before Frank and Gary came to pick me up.

"You two should spend some alone time together," I said. "I'll be gone, and no doubt Zach will be too, so why not take the opportunity?" My mother, quite rightly, smelled a rat.

"Why are you trying to get us out of the house?" she asked me. I hated it when her paranoia turned to perspicacity—in other words, when she was right.

"I'm not," I said. "I just think you two deserve a good time for once. Can't a daughter love her parents without getting the third degree?"

"Whose party are you going to?"

"It's the Key Club—a service organization; very outstanding in the community. It's an honor to be asked." (This was a whopper of a lie. The Key Club actually comprised some of the baddest boys in school.)

"Who asked you?"

"Frank, the varsity quarterback, and Gary, the basketball

center." I neglected to mention that Frank was Hispanic and Gary was black. My father wouldn't care a whit, but my mother . . .

"Do I know them?" she asked.

I scrambled for an answer. "I'm sure you've seen their pictures in the paper. They're always being photographed." This seemed to mollify her somewhat.

When Gary called up to get my address, I told him not to come to the door; that I would meet them outside by the lamppost at the end of the driveway. He didn't ask for an explanation.

That Saturday, I sniffed the laundry extra quick and finished up all my other chores and homework in time to fix an early supper for the entire family. Granted, this was highly unusual, as all I typically did in the kitchen was eat, but my mother and father and even Zach seemed pleased by my initiative. "Maybe she's finally developing a sense of domesticity," my mother said, sitting down to the table I'd carefully set, with two white roses from the backyard blooming at my mother's place.

Domesticity be damned. I was desperate. I hadn't succeeded in getting my parents out of the house, so I was after tryptophan, the amino acid that induces sleep. To that end, I'd fixed some huge turkey sandwiches, along with creamy mashed potatoes and banana milk shakes liberally spiked with rum. I'd doubled up on the vanilla extract to mask the alcohol. I turned the stereo on to the radio station that played soporific elevator music.

"Do we have to keep listening to that crap?" Zach said midway through the meal.

"I find it very soothing," my mother said, and to my delight, she yawned. It was contagious: Daddy yawned, then Zach, then me, the biggest and loudest of all.

My mother finished her milk shake and said, "That was delicious, Terri Lynn. It's a real pleasure to be waited on for a change."

I felt a little guilty at that, but only a teensy little bit. "Why don't you go in the den and put your feet up for a while?" I said. "I'll wash the dishes and clean up the kitchen."

"Thank you, sweetie pie," she said. The guilt-o-meter spiked again, but I didn't let it deter me.

After she and my father left, Zach came over to me while I was at the sink. "What are you up to?" he asked.

"None of your goddamned business. Go nap."

He yawned. "I think I will. But don't think you've got me conned."

I didn't—but still, by a quarter to eight, everyone but me was sound asleep. I'd had a snootful of Boone's Farm Strawberry Hill by then and was myself a trifle drowsy. I sat on the porch, waiting for Gary and Frank to show up, taking deep breaths of the crisp night air to wake me up. Every inhalation made me feel a little bit drunker.

I was just resting my eyes for a minute when I heard it: three shrieking *beep-beep-beeps*. Despite my careful instructions for our rendezvous, the idiots were honking. They might as well have struck a gong. Those three earsplitting beeps were a death knell: the demise of all my planning and scheming. The end of my dreams for "pretty enough."

I knew in a flash what was going to happen, but nonetheless

I scrambled to my feet. "Shhh!" I said as loudly as I dared and sprinted to the waiting car. I wasn't fast enough. Behind me, I could hear the creak of the front door opening. The voice I least wanted to hear at that moment cried out, "Where do you think you're going?"

The Black Beast wanted to keep on running, but I knew the jig was up. Reluctantly, I turned to face my mother.

"You know, the Key Club party," I said. "I didn't want to wake you."

"Who are these boys?" she asked. Gary and Frank were getting out of the car and coming up the driveway. Before I could introduce them, my mother ordered me back into the house. "Inside. Go. Now."

I watched all agog from the kitchen window as she said a few words to Gary and Frank. It was too dark to see the expressions on their faces, but they turned around, got in their car, and drove away. My mother came back inside.

"What did you do? What did you *do*?" I wailed. I was frantic and tipsy and having one hell of a time controlling the Black Beast, who wanted to rip out her throat. For an instant, the image of blood soaking into that perfectly starched white linen collar overwhelmed me. I had to sit down.

"I told them you couldn't go out tonight."

"How could you?" I started to sob.

"What's all the commotion about?" my father asked, emerging from the den sleepy-eyed.

"They're two of the most popular boys in school, and she ordered them off the property just because they're black and

Hispanic." My sobs were uncontrollable now, racking my body like hiccoughs.

"Julia, is this true?"

My mother examined her fingernails carefully. "You should have seen their car," she said.

True, Frank's car was a disreputable old Chevy with half the front bumper coming off, but that was a bullshit excuse. I knew it, the Black Beast knew it, and my father knew it too. I held my breath, waiting for justice to rain down from on high.

And waited.

"Remember, you agreed last week that I'd be in charge of her dating," my mother said.

"Yes, but—" my father said.

"Well, did you mean it, or was it just another one of your lies?"

My father glanced down. His cheeks were red. I put my whole heart into my eyes and silently begged him to do the right thing. He wouldn't look at me. And he didn't say a word.

I couldn't believe it. I ran toward the door. I had to get away from that sight: my mother exultant, my father clearly ashamed, but of what, I wasn't sure. Her prejudice? Or his passivity? Whatever the reason, I couldn't bear it one more minute. My hand was on the doorknob when my mother said, "Stop. You're grounded."

I was outraged. "For what?"

"I think you know," she said.

"No, I don't. Why don't you spell it out clearly, so all of us can hear?"

"Jack, you tell her she's not going out tonight."

"You're in charge of her dating," he said, and without another word, without a single glance at me, he went back into the den.

I felt dizzy, like the floor was sliding out from under me. I twisted the knob and flung open the door. I heard my mother shouting behind me, but as I stepped outside, her words were swallowed up by the wind. There was a Santa Ana blowing that night—hot, dry air straight from the desert, practically calling my name. I knew then where I needed to go. I needed the comfort of vast open spaces, far away from anyone, where I could break into little pieces, unseen.

I'd never disobeyed a direct order from my parents before. It was terrifying; for the first couple of blocks, I kept looking in my rearview mirror, expecting to see my mother chasing me down the street. The magnitude of what had happened hadn't really hit me yet. It took a few more miles before I realized the truth: my father, the only bulwark I had against all harm that might befall me, had not protected me. The man who had taught me about Martin Luther King, Jr., and even made me memorize the first part of his "I Have a Dream" speech, had allowed evil to prosper in his own home. He was not the man I thought he was, and I—I was suddenly not a child anymore. My parents were wrong, and I was right. Dead right.

There was something dreadfully exciting about being the only enlightened soul in the universe.

I'd instinctively taken the freeway east, heading toward the high desert. There was no other traffic at eight o'clock on a Saturday night on I-15. I had the entire road—the entire world, it seemed—to myself. I turned on the radio, loud. The music exploded into the empty air: "I'm pickin' up good vibrations / She's givin' me excitations . . ."

What flips the switch between mania and just a really great joyride? For me it was the sense of desperation pulsing through my body, like the beat behind the music. I felt as if I were fleeing terrors that became more real, more vivid, with each passing mile. The farther and the faster I drove, the more I felt like something was after me. And yet in spite of the fear, it was thrilling. Mania is always great grand fun, right up until that point when you exceed your limit.

I pulled the 'Vette over, put the top down, then hit the gas. I defy anyone with a drop of red blood in their veins to resist the Beach Boys on a Saturday night, with a Santa Ana wind streaming through your hair and a fuel-injected engine purring at your command. "Good, good, good / Good vibrations . . ." I'd been cruising thus far, but I gunned it up, to spite a passing speed limit sign.

Rules. What was the point of rules if in the end there was no justice? When I graduated from college, I'd go on to law school and become a famous lawyer. A real lawyer, who fought for equality and inalienable rights, like Atticus Finch in *To Kill a Mockingbird*. I'd make sure that the good rules were enforced, the bad rules were rescinded, and fairness always prevailed.

Then I thought about the lawyers I knew. They always had either a hangdog look or a subtle sneer, as if they had just smelled something bad. No, maybe not a lawyer. I'd be a famous writer instead, exposing the underbelly of discrimination, the corruption of hypocrisy, the cruelty of labels. Writers needed very few rules—just punctuation, grammar, and respect for the truth. In fact, the best ones lived outside the rules.

I passed another speed limit sign: sixty-five mph. Bah! I punched the accelerator, and the 'Vette responded instantly. Seventy-five, eighty . . . There was no one to see, and no one to care, and the wind felt like invisible fingers caressing my hair. I reached behind my seat and pulled out a bottle of Boone's Farm Strawberry Hill, which I always kept stashed there for emergencies. I knew it was against the law to drink and drive, but in the mood I was in, that hardly mattered. My contempt for the adult world and its meaningless prohibitions had never felt so deep and profound. I unscrewed the cap and took a long guzzle. The wine was warm and sweet, and I let it flow through my body.

Eighty-five, ninety . . .

Suburbia had completely disappeared. It was replaced by miles and miles of barren desert, as far as the eye could see. Just flat land and the occasional Joshua tree, junipers, and sagebrush. I wanted the road to go on forever. I was just the slightest bit woozy—my fingers and toes were tingling—and I was sure that if I could drive far enough, I'd hit the horizon and fall clean off the edge of the world. But the off-ramp for Hesperia was coming up soon, and I reluctantly slowed to take the turn.

There were no intersection lights back then, just a few isolated stop signs. I whizzed by the truck stop where Daddy and I always had chili; past the general store; and then, with a honk and a wave, past Custom Homes, with its bright and cheery red rock roof. There was little left to Main Street after that. I could see the skeletons of some of my father's homes emerging in the distance, but for the most part, it was just me, the road, and the occasional tumbleweed.

I pulled over and stopped, leaning my head back to drink in the zillions of stars and the rest of the Strawberry Hill. Night in the desert always made me feel tiny, like a pinprick in the endless embroidery of sky. Seeing Daddy's brave red roof had not had the effect I'd intended: it made me feel homesick. But what was there to go home to? And to whom? Was my father still my father now, or a stranger I had never really known?

The Black Beast, which had enjoyed the ride immensely thus far, grew irritated at the delay. My palms began to itch. "There's nothing for you back there," he said. "Keep moving. Faster. There's no time to lose. The answers are all ahead of you."

I threw the empty bottle as hard as I could at a nearby yucca tree. Another rule broken: good. The smash and tinkle were just what I needed to break me out of reverie. I pictured my mother's self-satisfied smile, and a flash of anger scorched my skin. The Black Beast was right. I couldn't go home. There was nowhere left for me to go but forward, faster, into the night.

I revved the engine. God, that growl: it was like an instant hit of adrenaline. Between that and the wine and the Black Beast's goading, I was feeling pretty high—so high I decided to push the 'Vette as far as it would go. I'd never really opened it up all the way before. I hadn't "red-lined the tach," as Zach and his car-crazy friends would say.

I noticed when I got back on the road that the white line in the middle looked blurry and indistinct. No doubt they'd run out of bright white paint this far into the desert. More likely, no one had cared. I tried to follow the wavy line, but it made me feel dizzy, so I just braced myself against my seat, put my foot on the accelerator and stomped down hard. I roared into second, did a quick power shift up into third, a short yank down to fourth, and I was flying. I left the wavy white line behind me and hydroplaned on the dust.

Ninety-five, one hundred . . .

Finally, life was moving almost fast enough to satisfy the Black Beast. My hair was whipping into my eyes, and it stung like the devil's lash. Without thinking, I took one hand off the wheel to brush it away. The car swerved crazily, and I almost lost control. I panicked for a second, but it righted itself, and I found the little white line again, the only marker of sanity in the blur that used to be the world.

One hundred and ten, one hundred and fifteen . . .

Not enough, not nearly enough. Speed was good, but speed without destination felt pointless, like I was simply spinning my wheels. But where was I to go? I'd left the house with only my keys. I had no money, no identification, and worst of all, no liquor left to fuel my journey. Besides, I was too old to run away from home. Over the whine of the engine, I heard a whisper: "You're never too old to die."

Suicide. Ah, suicide. The ultimate destination. I'd romanced it often enough throughout the years, but since my unsuccessful attempt at age seven, I'd never seriously tried it again. Now it wooed me like a long-lost love, insinuating itself inside my veins, infiltrating every pore until it was all that I could think of. Part of me was scared—so scared that I wanted to yank the wheel and pull a U-turn right there in the middle of the road. But a bigger part was exultant, as if I'd just solved an impossible equation in math. Suicide—such a lovely word, like a sweet kiss on the lips—was so clearly the answer.

But it was a much more difficult proposition now. At seven, I'd had access to my mother's pills. And far more importantly, I was convinced that when I died I'd go straight to Heaven. Now I wasn't so sure. Overall, like everyone else, I thought I'd led a pretty good life, especially considering all the temptations to misbehave that the Black Beast had put in my way. But was it good enough? Or did God require an A-plus?

One hundred and twenty, one hundred and twenty-five . . .

The steering wheel began to vibrate in my hands, and my thoughts outraced the speedometer. "Bless me, Father, for I have sinned." So many sins—too many to count. I could try to blame them all on the Black Beast, but I didn't think even God would understand that the Black Beast wasn't really me. Sure, he was a part of me, but not the part that I embraced as the essential Terri. He was an interloper, an unwelcome intruder who broke into my mind and forced me to do the strangest things. Like now: it wasn't me who was driving a hundred and twenty-five miles per hour down a deserted desert road in the middle of the night, with a bottle of booze in my bloodstream. The Black Beast had the wheel.

One hundred and thirty . . .

The wind was shouting so loud in my ears, it was hard to think, and even harder to plan. How could I possibly do it? I had no pills, no knife, no gun. I supposed that I could park the car and hitchhike, and maybe get picked up eventually by a homicidal maniac. But that seemed too long a shot, even for Hesperia. I knew there was a lake somewhere nearby, although I wasn't quite sure where. I could drive the 'Vette at full throttle into the water, but could you drown in a convertible? And besides, even if I was going to die, I didn't want to hurt my beloved car.

I had to laugh at the irony of this, and the sound of my laughter startled me back into something resembling sanity. How could I die, when I could still laugh? I was only sixteen, after all: there were many more tragedies and triumphs yet to come. I had friends who cared about me, family who—though deeply flawed—still loved me. No doubt my parents were both worried sick about where I was right now.

A hundred and thirty felt really good, but it was far too fast, too soon. I eased my foot off the accelerator and closed my eyes for a second to thank God for this brief kiss of clarity. It was the right thing to do, but the wrong time to pray.

The rock appeared out of nowhere, smack dab in the center of the road. I saw it too late to swerve. The sickening sound of crunching metal and shattering fiberglass filled the air, drowning out even the wind.

All I remember is spinning, spinning, off the road and onto the sand. I kept trying to scream, but the dust was too thick, and it choked me. I tried to remember my driver's ed class, which hadn't been so very long ago. What did it mean, "Steer into the spin"?

Was that left or right? It didn't matter; the wheel wouldn't respond. Then I must have hit another rock, because the car suddenly lurched forward and I slammed against the wheel. The black desert sky turned even blacker, the stars exploding inside my head.

When I came to, I was covered with blood. The stars had fled, and the sky was a pure and crystalline blue, the light so bright it hurt my eyes. I looked in the rearview mirror: there was a nasty gash across my chin and a lump on my forehead, but mercifully, the rest of my face had escaped unscathed. Not so the 'Vette. I shakily got out and examined the damage. There was a long, ragged tear along the left side, the front bumper was crumpled, and the left front tire was blown.

I looked around me. There was nothing but cacti and tumbleweeds stretching from here to eternity. I'd missed the dawn, so I didn't know which way was east or which was west. In a daze, I walked to the edge of the road and waited to be rescued. "Princess," my father used to call me. Princesses always got rescued.

Oddly enough, it was Zach that I wanted. Although we were not the closest of siblings, a big brother is still a big brother, and this was no time for parents. I'd call Rhonda, I thought, and she could call Zach, and Zach would come and save me. I had plenty of time to think and plan in the five or so hours that elapsed before the nice burly truck driver happened by. But it wasn't until I was in his cab, safe and relatively sound, that I finally started to cry. The two things that I loved best in the world—my perfect father and my shiny car—had been ripped asunder that night.

The 'Vette, I knew, could be repaired.

5

Looking, nowhere inside myself
Is there the break required
To admit to, or submit to,
Or to say their way is chosen.
For it's merely what they've chosen
Never knowing choice existed
Whereas I, who saw both consequence
And consequence, resisted.

—Age eighteen

When I made it back home, I was grounded for
life—or at least until my parents' tempers cooled down. I

wouldn't see the 'Vette again until my junior year; it took that
long to fix. By then I'd finally made varsity cheerleader, and I
missed out on all the fun I could have had with the car: circling
the football stadium with the squad on big game nights, cruising
in the homecoming parade.

I knew that the wreck was partly—mostly—my fault, but
for a long time I refused to accept full responsibility for that
terrible night in the desert. I blamed my mother and father
for forcing me into despair. I blamed God for suckering me
into prayer. And I blamed the Black Beast for not missing that
rock.

I forgave my father eventually, but I never saw him in quite
the same light again. The myth had been shattered: the lovely
bedtime story I'd been told my whole life, where I was the
blessed damsel and he was my constant knight, always there
to save me. I felt the disillusionment creeping over me like a
fungus. Overnight, the things I'd learned to love and trust had
turned vulnerable and corruptible.

And so, at seventeen I discovered the impotent glory of cyni-
cism. Or perhaps I just grew up. I'm not sure whether I actually
began to see things more clearly or whether a haze of dissatisfac-
tion clouded my sight. But everything—everything—seemed
dull and prosaic to me: my friends, my schoolwork, my writing,
my home, my life. I remember our rose beds were in spectacu-
lar bloom the year that I turned seventeen. I would sit on the
grass and pick them apart, petal by petal, wondering why I used
to adore them so. Now they seemed like yet another false front,
another lie obscuring the truth of what was really going on

inside our house. I felt so jaded by then, I couldn't even see the simple beauty in a flower.

I decided to try an experiment. For one whole day, I'd give the Black Beast full rein. Whatever he wanted to do, I'd do it. Whatever he felt like saying, I'd say it. No matter what happened, it had to be better than this slow death from boredom.

I chose the day of the Big Game: the Citrus Belt League football finals. Just one more win, and we'd be champions. But that night's game was going to be the hardest. It was against our biggest rival, the San Gorgonio Spartans, and the odds were against us. The Black Beast *hated* San Gorgonio. I sat on the edge of my bed and let hostility (and its favorite companion, grandiosity) infuse my heart. The Spartans always beat us in basketball, baseball, and water polo. I'd be damned if I was going to let them win tonight.

Sometimes the Black Beast's anger was so intense it made my hazel eyes glow green. I stoked it, recalling in vivid detail how the Spartans' cheerleaders had jeered at us last season. By the time I sat down at breakfast, my skin was flushed and tingly. I felt dangerously pretty.

"Good morning, baby," my father said. His voice was hoarse from a lingering cold. "Ready for the pep rally?"

I was in my orange and black cheerleading uniform, the pleated skirt so perilously short it verged on peekaboo. "You bet. I spent all last night perfecting our cheers. I'm going to *make* those boys win, whether they're good enough or not. Like you always told me, words are the most powerful things in the world."

"They'd better be," Zach said. "'Cause your quarterback's a wuss."

Normally, I tried to ignore Zach's barbs at breakfast. Not that morning. I grabbed my knife and fork and made a deliberate show of cutting and stabbing my pancakes with vigor. "Look, Zach," I said. "I've got utensils."

He blanched but didn't say anything. I held my fork up in the air and admired it. "You know, a fork is really an amazing thing. Every girl should carry one around with her for protection. It's simple, portable, and given enough provocation, probably lethal."

Zach snatched his book bag off the counter. "I'm late," he said, and fled. I stabbed another pancake with my fork. It tasted delicious.

That afternoon, I had lunch with the cheerleading squad. We were seated at the table way in the back, out of the eye line of the cafeteria helpers—the spot normally reserved for shady transactions (pot sales, mostly). Cheerleaders had far more social clout than stoners, so I was able to secure the table for us with a simple "Shoo!" and a wave of my hand. The stoners scattered like cockroaches.

With the other girls shielding me from sight, I dumped out a wad of money I had stuffed in my megaphone. "Wow!" was the unanimous reaction. There were piles of it: ones, fives, tens, and twenties. I started to count.

"If the teachers ever catch you at this, you know you'll be expelled," Allison, the head cheerleader, scolded me. She was the only one who could authorize collections, so she alone knew something fishy was going on. Allison had great big breasts and enormous cornflower eyes, which were opened even wider than normal at the sight of all that money. I decided right then and there that big breasts were vulgar, and innocence was annoying.

"Shut up," I said. "You made me lose count."

I'd spent the whole morning working the crowd at the pep rally. I was so convinced that our brilliant cheers were going to spur the Chaffey Tigers on to victory, I'd laid down odds on that night's game. While the other girls went through the choreographed routines, I'd passed amongst the spectators, handing out buttons and flags and stickers—ostensibly trying to rally school spirit but actually whispering, "I'll cover all bets on the game."

"But Terri—" Allison started to whine. The Black Beast shot her a look of such venom, she put her hand to her throat and was silent.

"What's wrong with collecting money for a good cause?" one of the other girls asked. "We do it all the time."

"There's nothing wrong with it," I said. Allison didn't contradict me.

Chaffey was a pretty big school: about four thousand students in all, and football was king. So a lot of kids came to the pep rallies, even if it was just to make fun of our cheers or peek up our skirts. Most of the students didn't have very much cash, but between their lunch and dope money, I'd managed to clear five hundred or so. Five hundred smackers. What was I going to do with it? It never even crossed my mind that we might lose, and I'd have to pay it all back—at two-to-one odds.

"We could use some new banners," one of the cheerleaders said. "Ours are getting pretty shabby."

"Or how about a deejay for the victory dance?" another asked.

The other girls started peppering me with their suggestions too, and I found myself growing increasingly irritable. It was my money, I'd collected it, and I'd do with it as I saw fit. I should have just gone into the girls' bathroom by myself and counted the money there. That was the problem with interacting with other people, especially stupid people who didn't know how to mind their own business.

The tag on the back of my sweater kept itching my skin. I scratched it so hard that my fingernails drew blood. Maybe I'd get a manicure at one of those fancy Beverly Hills salons or a proper haircut at Vidal Sassoon. And my father's birthday was coming up—I could buy him something extravagant, something he'd never expect. That watch we'd seen in the window of Van Cleef & Arpels: I knew how much he coveted it.

The girls were still arguing about this cause or that. The Black Beast had no time for such dithering. I swept the money back into my megaphone and got up with a curt "I've got to go study now." I stashed the megaphone in my locker and got out my book for the next class. History. Good. We were studying the Tudors, and Henry VIII's great lust for power appealed to me at that moment.

I didn't know what was the matter with me. I couldn't seem to concentrate on the slide show, even though it was about Henry VIII's wives, a subject that I usually found fascinating. (I always suspected that Anne Boleyn had a bit of the Black Beast in her too.) A fly kept buzzing around my desk, alighting briefly but never quite long enough for me to kill it. I swatted wildly at the empty air, the students around me giggling. Finally, the fly landed right on top of Alonzo Gonsalez's head, directly in front of me. I hefted my history textbook and slammed it down on his head. He turned and cursed me loudly. The teacher flicked on the lights.

"What's going on back there?"

"She hit me," Alonzo said.

"I did not," I said, sounding shocked. "I hit the fly. And there it is." I pointed to the belly-up fly that had wound up on my desk.

The teacher sighed. "Class, who was Henry VIII's first wife?"

I didn't even bother to raise my hand. "That's easy. Catherine of Aragon."

"And after that?"

Now it was my time to sigh. It was all too goddamned easy. "Anne Boleyn." Without further prompting, I reeled off the rest: "Then Jane Seymour, Anne of Cleves, Catherine Howard, and Katherine Parr."

"Excellent, Terri." The teacher turned the lights back off and resumed the slide show.

Alonzo was still angry at me. He turned around and whispered, "Show-off. Bet you're not even cool enough to touch that fly."

He knew, as did all the students who'd been in science class with me, that I was extremely queasy when it came to insects of any kind. Mere spider webs freaked me out; the sight of a scuttling black beetle could make me feel faint. I'd been excused from dissecting worms in Mr. Hamish's class on grounds of "acute palpitations."

But the Black Beast was bored, oh so terribly bored, and Alonzo's words had the ring of challenge to them. No, I said to myself. Not that. Please, not that. But I'd made a pact: whatever the Black Beast wanted to do . . . My hand reached out toward the fly. All the students around us were watching me now, as I picked up the dead fly by its disgusting wings and dangled it before Alonzo's astonished eyes. Then I slowly lowered it to my mouth, tilted my head back, and popped it in.

I actually swallowed it all in one gulp, but I made a big show of chewing and smacking my lips. "Yummy," I said, just before Alonzo spit up his gum. It was heaps more interesting than even Anne Boleyn, but it didn't satisfy the Black Beast's craving for more, and yet more, stimulation.

Underneath my profound boredom lay profound agitation, and underneath that, something darker still: a sense of slowly approaching doom. My skin felt so prickly, the tiny hairs on my arms seemed to be standing on end. I tried to sit still, but the Beast was too antsy. I kept shifting around and around in my seat, searching for a comfortable position. The girl sitting behind me complained, "Terri, stop fidgeting. I can't see the screen."

Asking the Black Beast not to fidget was like asking a tornado to stop whirling around. I tried to find the tornado's eye—calm, quiet, still—but all around me thoughts were spinning, ideas were pulsing, words were pushing up against my tongue, begging to be released. I grabbed my notebook and started scribbling, pressing the pen down so hard on the paper it tore right through the page.

"The Game."

I stared at my notebook, unaware that these two little words would eventually change my life. "The Game." What did it mean, and why had I written it? Understanding didn't matter. Expression was all. I started to write, the words pouring out of me, rhymes and rhythms and associations all jumbled up together like alphabet soup.

Only one early draft of "The Game" has survived, but I remember well the conceit: I suddenly realized that the integrity of everything around me was hanging by a thread, the tenuous thread of compliance. We had all agreed to play the same game and abide by the same largely unwritten rules. Teachers would teach, and students would listen; cheerleaders would always outrank stoners; stoners would always outrank nerds. Parties and proms mattered far more than politics, even in our tumultuous times. And good looks—not beauty; *never* beauty—could buy you the entire world.

When had I signed up for this? I hadn't. I knew in a flash of clarity that all I had to do was stand up and shout an obscenity, or do a bare-ass cartwheel in the aisle, or snap up all the window blinds to let the sun blaze through, and the whole carefully calculated structure would come tumbling down around my ears. The urge to do these things was strong, but the urge to write my revelations down was stronger still. I learned an important lesson that day: writing could sometimes calm the Black Beast. Much as he loved to incite and provoke, he adored the ecstasy of inspiration—the flow of words from ether to pen to page—even more.

History was the very last class of the day, and when the bell rang, I stayed behind and kept on writing. I wrote until my fingers cramped and my feet grew numb. Shadows crept across the room. I didn't stop, not even long enough to turn on the lights. There were just too many things to say. It was all a game, all of it: family, friendships, school, career, marriage, children, decline. I'd never asked for any of it. I'd just been plopped down in the center of the Monopoly board and expected to know my next move, because Monopoly was always played the same way. When in doubt, consult the rules. But nowhere in the rules did it say what to do if a player all at once decided that she didn't want to play anymore.

A little knowledge can be empowering, liberating, a giddy thrill. But too much knowledge, too soon, too young, can be a dangerous thing. I felt like I was seeing too clearly. The fabric of the universe was stretched out before me, and it was a pitiful sight: moth-eaten and threadbare. Now that my eyes were fully opened, how I longed to be blind again.

I wrote and wrote until the words began colliding on the page, and I couldn't make sense out of them anymore. I felt like a windup toy that had been wound too tight: I wanted to stop, but I couldn't. My hand kept writing the same seven words, first in flowing cursive, then in big block print, then in what looked like a child's careless crayon scrawl. I filled up several pages, then went back and wrote in between the lines, in teeny-tiny letters so small that I had to squint to see them. The same seven words, over and over and over again: "*I have to get out of here.*"

And the scary part was, I wasn't sure who was saying it: me or the Black Beast.

It was dark when I finally raised my head. The room was suffocatingly close, and I felt like I couldn't draw a decent breath. The writing fury had passed, and in its place was an exhaustion so profound that I wondered how I would ever get home again. I should call my parents, I thought, and tell them where I am. They weren't coming to the game because of my father's cold, and I knew they must be worried. But I sat there, not moving a muscle, too tired even to blink. I sat and stared at the words I had written. The words stared back at me, bold and true: *I have to get out of here.* Yes, but first I had to move.

I tried to raise my little finger. Impossible. Ring finger, middle finger, index, and thumb: not ten minutes ago, they'd been maniacally scribbling. Now they lay inert on the desk, dull and heavy as lead. My body wanted nothing whatsoever to do with my brain. The commands that I issued were simply ignored.

There may be more terrifying things than paralysis, but if there are, I don't know them. My skin was my prison. My veins and arteries were like barbed wire encircling my body, circumscribing my limits. Alcohol was the only thing that had ever helped me break free of this feeling, but the nearest drink was miles away.

I thought with a sudden staggering fondness of Stinky Pete, and the magical way he was able to transform mere money into a mood-altering elixir. How good he'd always been to me, always ready with a quip or a compliment as he handed me the brown bag. "You look mighty nice tonight, miss," he'd say, but I was so eager to get at the liquor, I never stopped to say anything kind in return. Just a hurried "thanks," and I was off to the next party, the next dance, the next big game that seemed so important to me at the time—far more important than a smelly old man's ragged attempts at civility.

The next big game. Jesus Christ. Panic jolted me out of paralysis, at least long enough to get up and open the window. Sure enough, I could hear the familiar strains of the Chaffey fight song in the distance. I looked at my watch: seven-fifteen. Kickoff was at seven.

I knew I should run to the stadium, but running was out of the question. I trudged to the pay phone at the end of the hall and called home. My father answered.

"Why aren't you at the game?" were the first words out of his mouth.

"I'm fine, thank you," I snapped. I never snapped at my father.

"Where are you?"

"At school. I was writing."

"Well, you'd better hurry," he said. "Kickoff was at seven."

"I know." I sighed. "Never be late to the game."

"That's right," he said. Then a beat. "Is there something wrong with you?"

It was the question I most wanted to hear and feared the most to answer. "Daddy, do I have to cheer tonight?" I asked, my voice so faint it almost evaporated.

"What are you talking about? It's the big game. Of course you have to cheer. Why, just this morning you said—"

"I know, I know." This morning felt like a lifetime ago. What had happened to that chipper cartwheeling cheerleader? Was she still alive inside my body, and was the Black Beast holding her hostage? I wondered what his ransom was. I'd pay any price, anything, just to be the very same person I'd been a dozen hours before.

"I'd better go," I whispered into the phone.

"Give 'em hell, baby," my father said, and then the line went dead.

I went to my locker, took out my megaphone, and began to stuff the five hundred dollars I'd collected into my backpack. It was a tight fit and seemed to take forever. There were so many loose bills—ones and fives and tens fluttering through my fingers—that I had to take out all my books and pens and papers to stash it all in. Two-to-one odds. Whatever had possessed me to offer that? If we lost—and now I was sure we were going to lose—I'd owe a thousand dollars. I didn't have a thousand dollars. I had three hundred or so in a savings account, maybe thirty more in my piggy bank. That left me six hundred seventy dollars in arrears. Even Daddy wouldn't fork over that large an amount without a damned good explanation.

At last, I managed to zip up my backpack, and made my way slowly to the football field. I had to concentrate on putting one foot after the other. It was a damp night, and the very air felt like it was resisting me, pushing back, impeding my forward progress. When I finally made it to the stadium, the game was in full swing. We were down by seven points.

"Where on earth have you been?" Allison demanded. "We had to do the fight song without you. It totally screwed up our rhythm."

"I'm sorry," I said. "I was—"

"It doesn't matter now. For God's sake, get in line and get going. We're already seven down."

"It's just a game, Allison," I said. She looked at me as if I'd gone mad.

Anyone who thinks cheerleading isn't a competitive sport hasn't been through Hell Week at USC: seven days in the blistering August heat, doing the same backbreaking routines over and over again, trying to get an edge on the neighboring teams before the real season starts. Our squad never won any awards, but we weren't that bad. We were blessed with several gymnasts, and the rest were natural athletes—strong and lithe and limber. I wasn't limber. At the moment, I felt barely alive.

Allison called out the next cheer: "Rock Steady!" Shit. Normally, I liked this cheer. In spite of its stupid words, it was full of sexy gyrations and a catchy rhythm that always got the crowd up onto its feet. All it consisted of was a few nonsensical lines: "Rock steady / What it is, what it is / Get down, get down / Goooooo, team!" But it was followed by our hardest stunt: the pyramid, where we threw Carrie, our smallest girl, high in the air and, hopefully, caught her on her way back down.

"Ready? Okay!" Allison shouted.

Thankfully, I was able to remember the words, since there weren't that many of them. But the moves? A cheerleader has to be thinking all the time of a dozen different things to make the routine quick and snappy: elbows locked, but never knees; arms stiff and fully extended; ab muscles tight; both wrists aligned; toes pointed, and so on. Constantly look to the left and the right without ever moving your head, to keep in perfect sync. Synchronization was next to godliness and second only to smiling. Smile, smile, until your jaw ached and your cheekbones felt like they were on fire. You *loved* this team! You *loved* to cheer! You knew that every girl out there was wishing she was you.

Since our school was so large, the crowds were huge. They made a mighty sound when they roared, like a tidal wave washing over me. I felt their eyes upon me, watching my every move. I owed it to them to sparkle bright, to infuse my body with such pep and vigor it radiated up into the stands, coercing even the most timid souls to clap their hands and stomp their feet and shout until their throats were raw. "Gooooo, team!" It was my job, and by God, I was going to do it if even if it killed me.

"Terri, smile!" Allison hissed.

I smiled. It hurt. Arguing furiously with my body, I mustered all the energy I could, threw my arms up into a V, and kicked my left foot—no, my right; no, fuck, my left—into the air, then I swiveled my hips and turned around. But I turned the wrong way and ran smack into the cheerleader next to me. She glared but kept on smiling, and I did the same, only now I was seriously off rhythm and couldn't catch the beat. I was cheering at thirty-three rpm, and the rest of the squad was at seventy-eight. I was slowly winding down into paralysis again. In the grand scheme of things, what did it matter which foot I kicked or which direction I twirled my ass?

We piled into the pyramid. I was left bottom anchor, which meant that I had to stay steady on my hands and knees while we balanced and tossed Carrie up in the air. But then I heard the other side yelling and clapping, and I knew they'd scored a touchdown again, and I just couldn't help it: I started to cry. If we lost, how would I ever get a thousand dollars together? Snot ran copiously from my nose, an infuriating tickle, and I automatically wiped it with my right hand, just as Carrie came hurtling down from the toss-up. The impact caught me by surprise, and I tried to brace, but I was moving too slowly, my mind too thick to react. My elbow buckled, and all at once there were seven cheerleaders on top of me, screaming. Carrie, fortunately, landed unhurt but was pissed as hell at me for weeks after that.

I pled injury—I told Allison I'd sprained my ankle. She had no choice but to excuse me from the rest of the game. I grabbed my backpack and surreptitiously hobbled toward an empty stretch of bleachers, far away on the other team's side, where no one could see me (or find me after the game was over and we'd lost and they all wanted to collect their money).

Time is an amusing thing when you're in the mood to be amused. I wasn't. I wanted instant relief, sudden certainty. But time is elastic as a Slinky toy, bending and stretching its way toward you at its own inexorable rhythm. I knew a little about the fickle nature of time: I lived, after all, at the whim of a Beast who often moved at lightning speed and then, at other times, refused to move at all. But that night, sitting and shivering in the opposing team's stands, waiting for the game to end, was surely one of the longest nights of my life. I kept checking my wristwatch, shaking it, holding it to my ear to make sure it was working. It was ticking, all right, and the scoreboard showed the minutes passing, but time just chuckled at that. It was slave to no man's machine.

So days and nights and eons passed, while the silly players in their silly uniforms did damage to a silly ball. Chaffey scored a few touchdowns, and even the Black Beast perked up his head at that and allowed me to feel a little hope. But then the other team scored again and again, and the Black Beast sank back down into despair. "Loser," he whispered, and the word went straight through me like the cold, cutting wind.

With less than two minutes to go in the fourth quarter, we were six points behind. Although I was still mad at God for wrecking my 'Vette, I knew that it was time to pray. I stared up into the mist-shrouded sky and searched for signs of life. A star— perhaps even a wisp of cloud—but no. The night was bleary-eyed and bruised, a dark purple mass of nothing. I put all of my faith and hope into a single prayer and aimed it at the emptiness: "Dearest God, I swear on my soul that if you get me out of this one last predicament, I will do exactly as you told me. I promise you: *I will get out of here.*"

As if on cue, a roar went up from the Chaffey stands. The fog had grown so thick by then that I couldn't see the field, and the scoreboard was a blur. I ran pell-mell down the bleachers, forgetting about my supposedly sprained ankle, and grabbed the nearest fan.

"What happened?"

"Goddamned Tigers scored a touchdown."

Then another roar: no doubt the kick, the extra point. I was close enough to see by then, a glorious sight: the Tigers hugging one another on the field, the cheerleaders jumping and scream-ing and doing herkies like mad, the Chaffey fans in a frenzy. I was saved. It was just a game, I knew it now, but Lord, how good it felt to win.

I didn't join the other cheerleaders. I hadn't earned the right to celebrate, and besides, I was no longer really one of them — half my heart was already out the door. I limped to my car, in case someone was looking, and drove away without speaking to anyone. On my way home, I stopped at the 7-Eleven. Stinky Pete was there, as always, huddling under his fortress of boxes in the back. He looked up as he saw my headlights approach. "Hey there, Missy, ain't you looking all spiffy in your cheerleader's outfit! So who won the big game tonight?"

"You did," I said, and handed him my bursting backpack.

College was the only clear means of escaping my life. I knew I had a nice little life compared to most, but that was the problem: it was little, and I wasn't satisfied. Not knowing what else to blame my ills on, I ascribed them all to suburbia, public high school, and my warped family dynamic (which I, of course, had done my best to create). Once I was as far away as possible from all of that, I thought, my future was unlimited.

As far away as possible meant the East Coast: the Ivy League or the Seven Sisters. So far as I knew, I was the only student in my entire graduating class of nearly a thousand who was desperate to go back East. It puzzled the Chaffey guidance counselor: "Why don't you just stay here and go to Pomona College?" she said. "You're sure to get a scholarship, given your past association with them." In frustration, I turned to Miss Miller, my mentor. She gave me the answer I sought: "Go and find yourself a bigger world. It's all out there, waiting for you."

I received an avalanche of college applications at the beginning of my senior year. I remember plowing through them with my father every night, making careful piles of yeses, nos, and maybes. As usual, Daddy wanted only the best for me, meaning instant visible status.

"Oberlin?" I asked.

"Never heard of it."

"Princeton?"

"Absolutely."

I was a little surprised by how eagerly he embraced the whole process, since it meant that I'd be leaving him for four years, and he would have to fight my mother alone. But any concerns he might have had on that score were apparently allayed by the prestige of having a daughter in a fancy Eastern college. He was giddy with anticipation, even excusing me from my usual chores because "she needs to focus," he told my mother, when she grumbled about having to do the dishes. Poor Zach, who was getting his own brand of higher education at Burger King in those days, inherited laundry duty.

My father had his agenda, I had mine. I searched through the applications for just the right one: the one that would serve as the complete antithesis to everything I now knew. Suburbia to me was a cheesy Hallmark card; I wanted engraved invitations to tea on gold-embossed stationery. Suburbia was leisure suits and bell-bottom jeans; I wanted white gloves and pearls, tweed and jodhpurs. I wanted to re-create the universe—not anew, but to go back in time to a more cultured, mannered, sophisticated era. I wanted, if possible, to leap forward into the past.

I had an excellent reason for seeking out time-honored tradition, beyond just its surface appeal. If I had learned anything from my life thus far, it was that my only real safety lay in a strong façade. Given my constant internal chaos, I needed a careful exterior. Something to divert the eye from what was really going on inside me—to contain and obscure the monster within. And then at last, after poring through countless applications, I found the perfect façade to hide behind: I wanted to be a Vassar girl.

I'd heard the phrase my entire life, "Oh, she's a Vassar girl," and the image immediately sprang to mind of a certain kind of woman: upper class, obviously, but with a streak of artistic bohemianism thrown in to make the palette interesting. I'd seen it often enough in the movies: Marilyn Monroe, for example, in *Some Like It Hot*, trying to pass herself off as a Vassar girl to impress pseudosocialite Tony Curtis. But it was more than just the moneyed allure that enthralled me. I thought of the alumnae:

Edna St. Vincent Millay, Mary McCarthy, Elizabeth Bishop, Meryl Streep, and so on. Jackie Kennedy went there for a while, even Jane Fonda. Impressive women all, and perhaps because my forays into dating had always been so disastrous, I had a very sketchy sense of myself as a woman. I could feel it, like a lacuna in my psyche.

At Vassar, it would be acceptable—no, necessary—to be a strong, intelligent woman. This was true, of course, of all the Seven Sisters schools, but in my mind there was an important distinction. While Bryn Mawr or Radcliffe might turn out a lady academic, Vassar would turn out a lady.

I pictured myself wearing sleek black cocktail gowns and drinking vodka martinis. It had not escaped my notice—indeed, it was a leading factor in my decision—that the drinking age in New York was eighteen. All the while, I'd be carrying on brilliant conversations with other men and women, for Vassar was coed by then, about wide-ranging subjects like art and politics and morals and poetry. It would be brittle and witty and just this side of risqué, for there was something slightly unsettling about a Vassar girl. She was different, a little bit dangerous, even; wild, at times unpredictable. I thought the Black Beast might find camouflage there.

And so began my single-minded pursuit of honor and glory— offerings to lay at Vassar's feet. Even though I had straight As and an extensive extracurricular record, I knew I'd have to do a lot more to catch the elitist admissions officers' eyes. I was, I realized, a nobody from nowhere. Big as Chaffey High School was, even I discounted it. Where was Ontario? Who was I? I took the

SAT exam as early as I could, then took it again until I achieved a near-perfect score.

If there was a contest anywhere, I entered it. If an honor was offered, I went for it. It was madness of a kind—a yearning for acclaim that knew no bounds or limits. My pursuit of romance fell by the wayside; I had little time for friends. My awards-seeking compulsion took precedence over everything. It was a life-or-death proposition, like hacking through Mordor.

I suspect I must have been manic—my soaring energy and ambition certainly suggest it. I didn't need sleep; I barely stopped for meals. And there was a synchronicity to my efforts: if I learned something one minute, I was able to apply it the next. Each new thought flowed into another, and another, and yet another, until there was a liquidity to the universe that I've since experienced only in full-blown mania. Everything connected.

But mania is a great exaggerator, so the teeniest, tiniest flux in my blood felt seismic. As a result, I was terrified the entire time—not so much of having to win as of having to be consistent. The necessity of constantly showing up on schedule for scholastic competitions was like one of my worst nightmares coming true. In the past, I'd never known which Terri would wake up on the day of an exam: the one with all the answers on the tip of her tongue or the one that could barely speak? The one with insight as crystalline as a Dutch still life, sharp and clear in every detail? Or the one whose mind was enshrouded by fog, thick and gray and impenetrable? Based on my past history, I knew I could succeed—I just didn't know if I would survive.

I decided to talk to my father about it. I remember one

night—I think it was before the big Bank of America competition—I went to him, trembling and very near tears. He was, as usual, nursing a scotch in his brown leather chair and smoking a Camel. He peered at me through the nicotine haze.

"Baby, what's wrong?" he asked.

"I don't think I can go through with it." He knew without asking what I meant.

"But it's your most prestigious event so far," he said. "Vassar will be very impressed when you win."

"I'm not going to win."

"Tell me one good reason why."

I wanted to let him in on my dilemma, but only so far. Our relationship hadn't healed to the point where I was willing to trust him with absolute truth. Besides, I didn't have words for the truth. I had to fumble for language we could both understand.

"There will be so many people there, and I truly don't know . . ." I faltered.

"You don't know what?"

"Who I'll be when I wake up tomorrow."

He looked puzzled. I decided to try another tack, a little further from the truth but still so close to the core that I turned beet red when I spoke the words.

"The thing is, Daddy, I'm terribly shy."

He laughed so hard that his face flushed too. "You? Shy? Honey, you're a born predator."

I knew he meant it as a compliment, but "predator" was so close to "beast," I got confused and was too scared to continue. Was it possible he had guessed the truth? Maybe the Black Beast had grown so strong, he was becoming visible. That was the last time I ever dared to speak to my father about my fear of competition.

Fortunately, I woke up the next morning on fire and eager to go. Which didn't mean the fear was gone; it was just lacquered in adrenaline and a fair amount of alcohol. I'd discovered that with just enough drink in me, I was passionate, effusive, enraptured by my subject. I spoke as if I meant every word, and for that brief spate of time in the spotlight, I did. I forget now what the Bank of America debate was all about, but it wouldn't have mattered to me back then. It didn't even matter which side I was on. "Resolved: The emancipation of women is the single most important event of our lifetimes" versus "Resolved: The emancipation of women is a misogynist slur." Who cared? I was an intellectual whore.

Every once in a while, I'd be unsteady on my feet, but I'm sure the judges just thought it was nerves. I never drank so much that I slurred my speech—only enough so that I could move my body freely, fiercely, through the field of battle, without fear of my *bête noire*, paralysis. It was odd and rather amazing how well I was able to control my alcohol intake when academic achievement was at stake, because whenever I drank socially, all that cautious self-control dissolved like the Certs I was forever sucking to mask my breath.

One drink at a party, and I'd be wide-eyed; two, I'd be amorous; three, I'd be your bestest friend, your long-lost soul mate and confidante; four, I'd want to tell the world how wonderful life was; five, the world was a vile place, and I was the worst of its inhabitants. I didn't have the tremendous capacity that I developed later on. At six or more drinks, I'd be spewing my guts out all over the neighbor's backyard or a convenient rosebush. But I never, in all my extravagant displays of social sloppiness, told anyone about the Black Beast. Some secrets are simply buried so deep that they can't even be thrown up.

During academic competitions, however—in what I later came to think of as my "professional drinking"—I limited myself to three or four deep swigs, max. I doubt that anyone even suspected I'd had a single drink. I just didn't look the type. Nineteen seventy-eight may have been a wild time for fashion, but I partook of no extremes: no mile-high platform shoes, no garish tie-dyes or fringed leather vests. I wore cautious suits and tailored separates, and I snipped my waist-long hair that year into the precisely manicured bob that I've clung to the rest of my life. In old photographs, I look like a lawyer-in-training (which, as it turns out, I was).

I soon amassed a great many honors, all the way from local-yokel commendations to National Merit Scholarship finalist. They looked great, piled up high on my bookshelves and spilling out onto my desk. But I was running my mind and body so hard that my mother became worried. She didn't share my father's rabid excitement about the prospect of my attending Vassar. She wanted me to stay close to home; she thought Pomona College would be ideal. One night she came into my bedroom while I was preparing for the next day's contest.

"Stop that for a few minutes and listen to me," she said, taking the pen out of my hand.

"I can't, I've got too much to do," I said, grabbing it back.

"You don't look well. You're losing weight, and there are circles under your eyes. I hear you up and about at all hours of the morning. Aren't you sleeping?"

With her mother's instinct and nurse's insight, she'd honed in on the truth, but I couldn't let her know, for fear she'd curtail my activities. Sleep had always been a big problem for me. When the Black Beast was in paralysis mode, I did nothing but sleep: days and days at a time of unwholesome, sweat-soaked, dream-heavy slumber that left me weary upon waking. But when he was in mission mode, as he was at that moment, I rarely slept. A quick snatch of an hour or two near morning seemed to suffice. I couldn't close my eyes any longer than that: there was too much to see to, too much to do.

What my mother couldn't know, because I did my best to keep them hidden from her, was that I'd begun to develop some troubling obsessive-compulsive tics. "Tics," at least, was what I called them, but no doubt that was putting it a bit mildly. On days when I was scheduled to compete, I could barely make it out of my room. I had to close the door, kneel down, and cross myself sixty-three consecutive times. (My lucky number, twenty-one, times my other lucky number, three.) All the while, I'd be saying a one-word prayer to Saint Jude, the patron saint of lost causes: "Please please please please please please please . . ."

The hardwood floor was so unforgiving, I had permanent bruises on both of my knees. If I forgot my count, I had to start again from the beginning. And then I had to repeat the whole ritual right before each competition, just to feel safe. So I spent a lot of time in strange bathrooms, down on my knees. If someone came in while I was doing my routine, I had to stop and do it all over again. I began showing up earlier and earlier to the events to make sure that I had time to "prepare," as I called it.

Alcohol, again, came to my rescue. I'm sure the tics would have been much worse without its soothing effect. I kept a bottle in my car at all times and fortified myself immediately before each contest, and during breaks, if possible. I didn't like to think about how much I was drinking. The few times that I did, usually in the midst of a horrific hangover, I rationalized to myself that others didn't have a Black Beast to pacify. When the Beast refused to let me move, I simply had no choice: I needed the drink to jump-start my body. It wasn't merriment, it was medicine.

And then once fluidity was restored, there would always be that moment—that single brief and shining moment—when I didn't feel despair. I didn't feel elation. I didn't feel much of anything, and for me the absence of constant, nagging emotion was a glorious sensation. At those times, alcohol didn't make me drunk, so far as I could tell. I think it made me normal.

The concept of "normal" had me stymied. I wanted it and despised it all at the same time. I didn't know, and I guess I never will, how much of my anguish was illness and how much was normal teenage angst. Certainly the intensity of my emotions, as compared to my friends', seemed way out of proportion, and the severity and rapidity of my mood swings were most peculiar. For a good part of my adolescence, I watched my friends and brother like a hawk, trying to mimic what seemed like normal reactions to various stimuli. *Oh,* I thought, *so this is how one does disappointed. This is how one does happy.*

But while they had desires, they didn't seem to yearn. They sought to achieve, but not to a frenzy. When they felt rejection, it eventually passed. They didn't wallow in sorrow as I did, prolonging it and nurturing it, reveling in the ecstasy of pure suffering. In short, their emotions appeared to me to be watered down, like the cheap wine that I drank so often.

My acute awareness that I wasn't normal was one of the reasons the essay portion of the Vassar application had me so concerned. It had to expose my inner core without hinting at the havoc that lay within. But how could I fully express myself without tipping off the admissions officers to my bizarre inner life? What if a whiff of the Black Beast came through?

Once again, Miss Miller inspired me. "Why don't you give them 'The Game'?" she suggested. In a moment of semi-sloshed bravery, I'd shared bits and pieces of it with her, but I'd never shown the entire thing to anyone, not even my father. It made me feel too raw, too naked—like Dorian Gray face to face with his portrait. But I was a little bit in love with Vassar by then, and it seems that whenever I am in love, I can't help but serve up my heart. So I typed up "The Game," gave a copy to Miss Miller, and submitted it with my application.

The end, or so I thought. But no: Miss Miller mimeographed

"The Game" and, with my reluctant permission, handed it out to all her classes. It became something of a cause célèbre, and for the first time in my life, I was popular for a reason that had nothing to do with the usual trappings of popularity: good looks, money, or social connections.

"The Game" was only a few pages long, but it was alive; it bristled with indignation. I'd tapped into something universal in adolescence: anger at the status quo and a dawning realization that life was not going to work unless and until one played by the rules. It was those rules that I really raged against—who made them up, and where was I when they'd been put to the vote?

Why, for example, did I have to spend an hour every morning putting on mascara, curling my hair, picking out just the right outfit, all in a vain attempt to be "pretty"? Why did pretty matter at all? Why wasn't ugly ever given its due? Even I, who'd always hated ugliness so much, had evolved enough in the past few years to realize that every ugly person had something unique: a certain lack of symmetry that ought to be celebrated, not reviled. True beauty could never lie in conformity. Conformity wasn't beautiful, because it wasn't brave.

The piece ended on a disturbing note—disturbing in retrospect, but written rather matter-of-factly at the time. The only draft I retain reads:

> I am bored, I am tired. My muscles ache with every movement,
> and I can no longer muster intensity for such a trivial little game.
> I seek a challenge, a freshness—the next level of competition.

Unfortunately, it's not to be found on these playing fields, and so I shall move on. The best players always move on, or else stop playing altogether. Which is perhaps the smartest move of all.

I think it was the first true suicide note I'd ever written, even though I had no concrete plan. I simply knew that I had to get out of there somehow, even if "somehow" meant death.

It was the misfit in me reaching out to the masses, and the masses responded. People I'd never seen before, never even knew existed, came up to me in between classes to tell me how much they'd loved what I'd written. Fat kids, skinny kids, kids from the chess club and the math club and the marching band—these, perhaps, I'd expected to get it. What astonished me was how many of the popular kids also seemed to under-stand. Bobbie Brandon, who'd been voted Prettiest Girl three years in a row, sat down next to me at lunch.

"Your story was really neat," she said, and her articulation ended there, but the tears in her turquoise-shadowed eyes spoke volumes. Even Elisa, who hadn't said a word to me since the whole Bob Greene fiasco, stopped me on the way to English class and gave me a big hug.

"I know exactly what you mean," she said.

It was a heady experience, feeling understood: one of, not one apart. Headier still was the knowledge that I could move my world with words.

For a week, nobody could touch me. I was soaring, high as a fighter kite, and twice as full of big blue sky. Human beings weren't so bad after all. They'd just needed a push in the right direction. A warm sense of belonging suffused my body; I could feel its glow upon my skin. When I looked in the mirror, for once I didn't see flaws. I saw a face—just a face, like any other: two eyes, a nose, and a mouth that wouldn't stop smiling. "Look at me, I'm one of you!" I wanted to shout to anyone who could hear me.

I decided to put "The Game" to a test. If everyone really believed that the rules were absurd, then they wouldn't mind breaking a few. For starters, Student Council elections. I'd been in student government for as long as I could remember, and it had always bothered me that there wasn't equal representation on the Council. What we had was a group of the most popular kids ruling the school, as always. Who spoke for the untouchables, the invisibles, who didn't hang out by the tiger?

For a week, I coolly canvassed the school. I checked out areas where the invisibles gathered: the dying shade tree by the gymnasium, the dirt field in back of the clock tower, the smelly old lockers near the bathrooms. I sauntered by as if on my way to more important places, but really I was eavesdropping furiously on their conversations, memorizing their appearances, sizing them up. I needed just the right accomplice.

Teena, cruelly nicknamed "Tiny Teena," was it. She was in my advanced French class. I knew she was there not because we were friends but because you simply couldn't miss her. She was, to put it politely, a big girl: big-boned and blubbery, with long, mousy brown hair that hung like curtains in front of her face.

We'd never talked outside of class. We lived in totally different worlds—both torturous, no doubt, but at least mine had the advantage of surface acceptability.

Whenever I saw Tiny Teena on campus, she was by herself: sitting in a corner of the cafeteria with a heavily laden tray of food, munching steadily, seemingly oblivious to the stares and snickers directed her way. I admired her sangfroid, if that's what it was, although I would never in a million years have traded places with her. Or even sat next to her in no-man's-land.

But while Teena may have sat by herself, she was hardly alone. There were far more students like her than like me, or Elisa, or Rhonda, or any of the other kids on the Council. The only equitable solution seemed obvious: Tiny Teena should rule the school.

I approached her after French class. To my surprise, she spoke to me first. "I really loved that thing you wrote," she said, a self-conscious blush suffusing her cheeks and making her look almost pretty. "It made me cry."

"I'm glad it touched you," I said. "Because I've got a proposition. I want to run you for Student Council."

Her mouth dropped open, and she stammered, "But how—but why—"

"I'm going to resign as senator and back you as my successor. There will have to be an election, of course, but I'm sure that with my help you'll win. Here's what we're going to do."

I didn't wait for her to say yes or even to take it all in. I reeled off a list of strategies: key people that we'd have to win over;

things we'd have to prepare—banners, flyers, posters, pins. The Black Beast was so enthused by this plan that the words simply flew from my mouth. I knew I was talking way too fast when a bit of my spittle hit Teena in the cheek, and she didn't even flinch. She just stared at me dumbfounded.

I tried to slow down but couldn't. My mind was running at hyperspeed by then, seeing the obstacles and dodging them, ricocheting from idea to idea like an amped-up pinball machine.

"So then you'll have to give your speech—"

"There's got to be a speech?" Teena asked, her eyes widening in horror. I'd never noticed before: she had lovely blue eyes, the color and, at the moment, the size of Dresden teacups. Note to self: buy navy blue liner to accentuate them.

"Don't worry, you'll be great," I said. "I'll write the speech myself. The message will be—what will it be? Wait, wait, don't tell me, I know! We'll use 'The Game' as our theme: 'Tired of playing by the rules? Vote for Teena and make a cheerleader cry.'"

Teena's face finally unfroze at that, and she laughed. "But you're one of *them*. Why would you do that? And why pick me?"

The Black Beast spoke before I could soften the words. "Because I'm sick to death of the way things are. And you're the last person in the world they'd ever expect to win."

Understanding dawned in those china-blue eyes, and damn it, they misted over.

"Teena, wait. I didn't mean—"

"Yes you did, and you're right. I'm always the last person anyone ever thinks of."

"Well, you won't be after this. We'll show them, Teena. We'll show them all."

Teena came over to my house the next night, and we set up camp out in the little shed behind the swimming pool. I'd decided to announce my resignation from the Council at the end of the week; that would give us several days of advance preparation to use to our advantage. I had lots of supplies left over from past elections—poster board, paper, balloons—so it was a breeze to churn out campaign materials. Except that Teena, perhaps befitting her size, moved slower than molasses. She did beautiful calligraphy, and while her posters outshone mine aesthetically, I did twenty to her one.

Granted, mine were slapdash affairs. As the evening wore on, I gave the Black Beast greater and greater artistic license. He favored crayons over poster paint because there was a better selection of colors. I swear, he must have used every single one in the deluxe-size pack. He didn't care if the colors clashed—in fact, I think he preferred it that way. As opposed to Teena's discreet and careful lettering, mine consisted of quick, bold slashes of wild hues piled one on top of the other for a vivid starburst effect. If van Gogh in one of his sunflower moods had ever painted Student Council posters, they might have looked something like this.

Teena was exhausted by ten o'clock, and I reluctantly let her go home. The Black Beast was just gearing up for the night. After my parents went to bed, I snuck back out and kept on painting feverishly by the eerie green light of the swimming pool. When dawn broke, I looked up and smiled. Its garish effects had nothing on me.

Teena came over the next night, and the next. We didn't talk much — just slaved over our banners and flyers and pins. But I came to like her placid, quiet company. It was such a blessed contrast to the frenetic metronome that kept ticking in my brain: what next, what next, what next?

By the end of the week, we had everything ready: enough paper to plaster the entire school. I went over and over the campaign in my mind and couldn't think of anything I'd left out, except perhaps the most important thing: I'd forgotten to swear Teena to silence. I didn't think I'd have to explain to her that our advantage lay in shock and surprise. And more truthfully, I didn't think she had anyone to tell.

But even Tiny Teena had friends of a sort, or acquaintances, among the invisibles. She apparently told a few of these about our scheme, and as plankton will eventually find the whale, so the rumor floated up and up the social food chain until it finally reached the Mauna Loas' ears.

Rhonda was the first to enlighten me. My father had to tear me away from the posters to answer the phone.

"Terri, I hate to tell you this, but . . ." Rhonda paused, and I steeled myself. "Everyone knows about the Tiny Teena thing."

Another pause. I held my breath.

"And they're all laughing at you."

The world, which had been spinning in such delicious, dizzying circles, suddenly stopped. "But they loved 'The Game,'" I said. "They told me so. I thought they were ready—no, eager—for change."

"That was literature. This is real life."

"But Elisa said—and Bobbie Brandon—"

"You're poaching on their territory. Come on, they're animals. We all are. Even you."

I thought of the Black Beast and couldn't disagree. I started to cry, quietly, so Rhonda couldn't hear me. "What am I going to do?" I asked, in a voice so soft Rhonda had to ask me to repeat myself.

"I promised Teena," I said. "She's really nice. Maybe if you could just get to know her . . ."

"Unpromise her," Rhonda said. "Tell her you're sick. You're always sick. She'll believe you."

I looked around me at the posters stacked up all over the den. "But everything's done. We've worked so hard, and she really thinks—"

"You don't understand how serious this is," Rhonda replied. "They're talking about impeaching you as president of the Mauna Loas."

The tears continued to flow down my face, my neck. I didn't even bother to wipe them away. I was stunned by my response, or rather, the lack of it: where was the anger, where was the rage? Where was the Black Beast's righteous indignation when I so justly needed it? It was nowhere to be found. All I felt was defeat and a desperate lethargy. Please God, anything but that.

"Thanks for telling me," I said. "I'd better go think."

As I hung up the phone, I was aware of how heavy the

receiver was; how difficult it was just to move my hand from my ear to the cradle. The air felt thick with betrayal. Without the Black Beast's frantic energy to sustain me, I knew I could never pull off this stunt—it required a kind of antic wit and defiance that didn't exist without him. I felt so frustrated, I wanted to scream. Why, when I most needed him, was he never there? Why couldn't I just summon him up at will, like Aladdin with his omnipotent genie? But the Black Beast was no fairy-tale friend. He was real and therefore capricious.

I called up Teena. I knew I had to rip this moment off like a bandage, while I could still move. "Teena, I'm terribly sorry, but there's been a hitch," I said, making my voice hoarse and low. "I'm coming down with something—the flu, I think. I won't be able to write your speech."

"But how can I do it without you?" She sounded panicked, and I sank lower into the sludge of shame.

"I'm sure you can manage. You know all our critical arguments: it's time for new blood, the world is ready, our school can stand as a shining example of fair representation . . ." My voice trailed off. I couldn't even convince myself.

Teena's voice grew hoarse as my own. I could tell that she was crying. "I don't want to do this if you're not going to be at my side."

"I can't be at your side forever. If you won, you'd have to act alone."

She was quiet for a minute. "I never really thought of that. I thought you'd always be there helping me, coaching me. I'm nothing when I'm alone."

"You're not nothing," I said. "You're the bravest girl I know." And then there was silence between us; a silence that lasted so long I knew it was the end of all hope—for me, for Teena, for social change, for personal redemption.

Teena snuffled and blew her nose. "Maybe this wasn't such a good idea after all."

It was my out, and I took it, knowing that I would despise myself forever, but unable to stop. I heard my words as if from far away. "Yeah, I guess maybe you're right." The nasty laughter that had been echoing in my ears finally stopped. I breathed a sigh of relief.

"Of course, we'll still be friends," I said. "You can come over anytime." We both knew that would never happen. Teena graciously thanked me and said good-bye. I curled up on the couch and tried to stop the tide of painful thoughts. It was no use. The dam was cracked, and they came flooding in.

Was this the kind of friend I was? Unreliable? Untrustworthy? Would I always be at the mercy of the Black Beast, unable to show up as I'd promised unless he was in the right kind of mood? Most of the sorrow in my life had come from unreliability: my father's failure to live up to my ideals, my mother's unpredictable storms. Now here I was, as guilty as either one of them.

I looked ahead into my future and saw an endless string of failed relationships: friendships I would surely sabotage, love I couldn't commit to. What in God's name was wrong with me? It would be so easy just to blame it all on the Black Beast, but some speck of honor, some modicum of truth, wouldn't let me do that. I truly didn't know how much of it was him and how much was simply me—a tragic character flaw that kept me trapped in infidelity.

I fell asleep, wishing I was anyone else, even Tiny Teena.

There was, of course, no election. No speech. I didn't resign my seat on the Council. I showed up every week as usual, but something essential had been extinguished in me: that spark that really cared one way or the other how the school should be run.

My retreat from the world was longer this time and more subtle than before. I stayed home as much as possible, but not for such lengthy periods that anyone got really alarmed. The teachers were used to my frequent absences by then, as were my parents. So long as I turned in my homework and showed up for exams, I could basically do what I liked.

Which posed a significant problem for me: I didn't know what I liked. Nothing appealed. It was verging on springtime, and I took long walks around the neighborhood, watching my favorite trees and flowers beginning to blossom back to life. I envied them their certain cycles. I had no idea how long this particular "spell" would last. A week? A month? Two months? Three? Graduation wasn't all that far away, but I was incapable of looking forward to it with any semblance of joy. It was just another red mark on the calendar, another day to be endured.

I was cool and distant to my friends, and they eventually stopped calling. But Rhonda still checked in most nights to tell me who'd done what to whom. I avoided her calls as much as I could, except when my parents were home and made me pick up the phone.

"Elisa and Bob Greene broke up today," Rhonda told me one early April evening. I'd been methodically picking the raisins out of the raisin bran, and this interested me just long enough to stop.

"How come?" I asked.

"A twist on what he did to you—except this time he told everyone how lousy Elisa was in bed."

I wanted to chuckle, but my chuckle mechanism wasn't working. My brain tugged at the corners of my mouth, trying to lift them into a smile; but that was just too much hard work, and so I sighed instead. Sighs came easily to me those days.

"What difference does it make now?" I said.

"Don't you at least think it's funny? The same exact thing, except backward? I laughed the whole way home."

"It's ironic funny, not ha-ha funny."

"Nothing's ha-ha funny to you anymore. I think there's something wrong with you."

There it was, my favorite phrase. I knew I should be mortified, even angry. But I listened dispassionately to Rhonda's words, wondering why they, like everything else, just didn't seem to matter.

"Sorry," I mumbled. "I guess I'm tired."

"Why? What did you do all day?"

"Slept."

"That's it?"

"And read some Sherlock Holmes."

"Enough with the Sherlock Holmes already. You need to get out of the nineteenth century. Come party with me this weekend. Bob Greene's throwing another bash, to celebrate his freedom."

"Not interested," I said.

This time Rhonda sighed. I could tell her patience was wearing thin, and to the extent that I could feel anything, it worried me. I had few enough friends left; I couldn't afford to alienate her. But it never once occurred to me to tell her I was scared. If she was annoyed with me now, imagine how disgusted she'd be to learn that her best friend was nothing more than the weak-souled slave of a Beast.

A few days later, my mother called me into her room, an event that happened infrequently enough that I felt a faint stirring of curiosity. She was getting ready to go out with my father and had laid out her long string of pearls on the bed.

"Here," she said, handing them to me. "Untangle those while I put on my stockings."

It was just like old times, and there was just enough little girl left in me to be thrilled by the touch of the milky-white pearls, so smooth and silky in my hands. I deftly picked through the knots, then held them out to my mother.

"You can put them on me," she said, which surprised me because she'd never let me do that before. I'd tried to, often enough, but she never seemed to like me touching the nape of her neck. "You're tickling me," she'd always say, then take the clasp out of my fingers and fasten it herself.

She sat down at her vanity and started brushing her hair.

Although she was nearing fifty by then, her hair was blonde and lustrous. She'd kept her figure too, and for maybe the hundredth time or so, I marveled at how her full breasts tapered into such a tiny wasp waist. Although I'd turned eighteen a few months back, I was still just a slip of a girl compared to her, with no real curves to speak of. And pale—so pale next to her lightly bronzed skin and vibrant lips, which still, after all these years, bloomed cherry-blossom red. I turned away from the mirror.

"No, look at me," she said. Our eyes met in the glass, and she spoke to my reflection.

"Rhonda called me yesterday," she said. "She told me she was concerned about you. I know you've missed a lot of school, but she said that even when you're there, it's like you're not really present. She said you're like a ghost. And I know that all you do around here is mope and read all day. What's going on?"

Few enough honest words had been exchanged between me and my mother that I remember these all too well. I dropped my eyes down to my shoes—a brand new pair of cork-heeled sandals, which I could never bear to wear again—and answered her as best I could.

"I don't know," I said. "It's like I'm numb. I can't feel anything except the bad stuff."

"Look at me," she said again. "I think you may need to see someone."

"You mean, like a doctor? But I'm not sick."

"Not that kind of doctor." Now it was her turn to drop her eyes.

The Black Beast, which had been laying dormant, suddenly snarled to life. An electric tingle shot through my body, as if I'd touched an open socket. My face flushed, and I could feel the blood rush through my veins. The sensations were extreme and unpleasant, yet even in the midst of them, I thought how absolutely wonderful to feel alive again.

"You mean a shrink? You think I'm crazy?"

Anger has never looked good on me. My skin gets red and blotchy, and my eyes narrow into slits. I hated seeing myself like that, but my mother had lifted her eyes to mine, and I was trapped inside the mirror.

"No, I don't think you're crazy," she said. "But I do think there's something wrong with you. Maybe a doctor can help. I've asked around, and—"

But the Black Beast wouldn't stand for any more of this. He wouldn't be caught, not after all these years, not by her or a doctor or anyone else. I tore my eyes away and ran out of the room, slamming the door behind me. It was the last time I was ever invited into my mother's private sanctum.

I threw myself down on my bed and fumed and kicked the covers. Here it was at last, the moment I'd always wanted: a chance to find out what was "wrong with me." But now that it had finally arrived, the truth was, I was too terrified. I was seven years old all over again, certain I'd be carted away in an ambulance, or a straitjacket, or something worse, and my father would cease to love me. Plus, what would I possibly say to a doctor? The reality of my situation was just too bizarre, the feelings far too inchoate to ever be put into words. I knew; I'd tried in my poetry, and even the comforting confines of rhyme couldn't rein in the blackness of my Beast.

Toto was lying on my pillow, and I hugged him tight, then threw him hard against the wall. "What good are you?" I shouted, not sure whom I was shouting at: Toto, the Black Beast, or God. "You don't protect me against anything."

The next moment I was down on my knees, sobbing, gathering Toto up in my arms and begging his—or someone's—forgiveness. My tantrum had ripped apart one of his fragile seams. I got my sewing kit out of my closet and tried to thread a needle with the special golden yellow thread I always used for Toto's wounds. But my hands were shaking too badly to aim, and I ended up stabbing myself with the needle.

The pain felt good: appropriate to the moment. So I pricked the tip of each finger, then the tip of each toe. But I wasn't going deep enough. I stabbed again, more viciously, until little droplets of blood oozed out. They were dark ruby red, almost purple. Like royal blood, I thought. I used to be her little princess, and now she thinks I'm insane. I ground the needle deeper still until the blood began to flow. At last, a queer serenity began to settle over me.

"Don't worry, tomorrow we'll run," I reassured the Black Beast, then leaned back and let the blood soothe me to sleep.

But tomorrow never came—at least, not the tomorrow I was expecting. The next morning, my father came running into my room with the mail. "It's here!" he said, and so it was, in neat, precise calligraphy: *Vassar College, Office of Admissions*.

"You open it," I said, hiding my bloodstained fingers under the bedspread.

He snatched the letter opener off my desk and slit the

envelope in one quick rip. His hands were trembling, and then his voice, as he read the six most glorious words in the English lexicon: "We are very pleased to announce . . ."

I felt a sharp flutter, which should have been joy but was, in fact, relief. At last, I thought. Escape. And just in the very nick of time.

Watching my father's ecstasy was almost as good as having some of my own. He simply couldn't contain himself. "Julia!" he bellowed. "We're in!" Then he grabbed me in a big bear hug and squeezed me so tight I was afraid my own fragile seams would burst. My mother came running in. "Let me see, let me see!" She was followed a moment later by Zach, who had an odd look on his face but said, politely enough, "Congratulations, Terri Lynn."

None of them noticed my bloody hands.

Everything happened so fast after that. Acceptance letters came pouring in from other colleges, I received numerous end-of-the-year awards, and the senior class voted me Most Likely to Succeed. My parents basked in the secondhand glory: how proud you must be, what a good job you've done, and what a fine family we were. "We always knew she'd do well," my father told the mailman, puffing out his chest and trying hard to sound humble. "But we never expected anything like this." My mother gave me second helpings of mashed potatoes without my even asking, beaming as she spooned them onto my plate. Even Zach stopped kicking me under the table.

I alone was untouched by the furor. I was pleased, of course, by all the offers and awards, but it didn't make much of a difference in my dreary mood. The Black Beast continued to mope and whine. "You'll never get out of here soon enough," he said, even as I crossed the rapidly diminishing days till graduation off my calendar with an emphatic red X. Only one thing broke through my veil of gloom: the subject of my mental health seemed to have been dropped for good, now that my future appeared assured. There was no more talk about doctors or shrinks, or anything being "wrong" with me—only kudos and congratulations and expressions of joy from all my teachers, my friends, and even the neighbors. The one time my mother tentatively said, "Remember what we talked about the other day . . ." my father shot her such a look, it could have killed a cobra midstrike. She didn't say another word.

Shortly after I accepted Vassar's offer, Principal Osder called me into his office.

"There were several ties for valedictorian, and the graduation committee has selected you to speak at this year's ceremony," he said. "Congratulations, Terri. We're all so proud of you."

It was a very big deal to be valedictorian, not just because of the large size of our class but because for the first time ever, the speeches were going to be broadcast live by a local TV station. The news caught me off guard, and while I mimed the appropriate gratitude, I struggled to figure out how I actually felt about this. I'd been so disillusioned by the whole Tiny Teena debacle, I honestly didn't know how much more I had left to give to the school. Part of me was just plain tired of performing, or maybe just plain tired; and I'd hoped that my graduation would be a fun, stress-free affair. A celebration, for once, a chance to kick back and party, not another mad scramble for the spotlight. For a moment—just a heartbeat, really—I considered saying no. But the Black Beast spoke up, loud and clear.

"Don't you dare!" he said, and while I wasn't exactly sure why he said this, his voice was so adamant, his tone so insistent, I smiled at Principal Osder and said, "Thank you, sir. I'm truly honored."

My father, of course, was thrilled to pieces when I came home and told him the news. "Great, that gives us three whole weeks to work on your speech. We'll make it letter-perfect," he said.

He looked so happy. What were a few more words, a clever turn of phrase or two, another bright light in my eyes, if it could bring him so much pleasure? I got out my three-by-five cards and waited for inspiration to strike. But the only words I could come up with were those same old well-worn seven: "I have to get out of here." Hardly the makings of an inspirational speech.

Finally, I pulled out my thesaurus and jotted down all the polysyllabic words that struck my fancy, thinking that perhaps if I wowed the audience with my erudition, they wouldn't notice that I had nothing to say. Throughout the following weeks, I piled on all the synonyms I could think of for every trite concept expected of a commencement speech: auspicious, propitious, roseate, utopian, and so on. I rifled through my myriad books of quotations, squinting at the tiny print for hours at a time, coughing up a little Longfellow here (". . . the great world of light, that lies behind all human destinies") and a little Churchill there ("This is not the end. It is not even the beginning of the end. But it is, perhaps, the end of the beginning").

I bored myself sick with valor and hope. My father hung on every word.

You would think that hours of poring through awe-inspiring quotes would at least have lifted my sagging spirits. But no. As is always the danger with browsing through books, I was constantly diverted by other words better suited to my real mood. The Black Beast kept pointing out other quotes: "Use that one! No, that one! That one is perfect!" He was a continual buzz inside my head, like one of those wildly fornicating mosquitoes Galway Kinnell had described in his poem. I simply couldn't ignore him. I'd try to copy down something uplifting, but the pencil would jerk out of control, or else my hand would just lie there, inert.

Longfellow may have been lilting, but Nietzsche was only a few pages away, calling hope "the worst of all evils, because it prolongs the torments of man." And for every good old Churchill soldiering on, there was a Voltaire decrying "the mania of maintaining that everything is well when we are wretched." I couldn't help it; these *were* perfect quotes, echoing exactly what I felt. I eventually gave up and just jotted down everything that the Black Beast liked and threw all those cards in a separate pile. What for? I didn't know. It made me feel so queasy, I had to put the book of quotes away and go ask my mother for some Pepto-Bismol.

Actually writing the speech was easier because it was just like sitting at our dinner table: I said everything except what was really going on inside. But I felt worse and worse with every word until, finally, I told my father I was done; I just couldn't write anymore.

"Do you think it's the best speech you've ever written?" he asked.

"No."

"Then you're not really done with it, are you?" He pushed the speech back into my hands. It lay there like a dead white whale, stinking up the place.

Despite the torpor of my words, despite the sluggishness of my intellect, tomorrows crept, as tomorrows will, until at last the Big Day arrived. It was a bad hair day. It was a bad skin day. It was a bad day all around. To get me going, I knocked back several slugs of the Strawberry Hill I kept hidden in my closet— not enough to make me drunk but enough to face the mirror. It didn't help.

I gave up trying to coax a curl out of my hair and just slicked it back behind my ears. The black cap and gown made the most of the dark purple circles that rimmed my eyes. I couldn't remember the last time I'd really slept, without visions of steel traps and cages chasing me.

"Terri Lynn, don't you maybe want to put on a little more blush? You look rather pale," my mother said as I walked into the kitchen.

"What for?" I asked, pushing aside the plate of toast and scrambled eggs she had fixed for me.

"So you look nice for all the people."

"We're all walking corpses. I might as well look like one."

"Suit yourself, dear. But there will be pictures, you know."

I knew, I knew. I was sick to death of everyone asking me if the TV cameras were going to make me nervous. Nervous would have required some spark of animation in my body. The extra publicity was fine with me—maybe they'd cover my funeral too: "Valedictorian kills herself after stunning oration. Family, friends distraught. City mourns. Film at eleven."

But by the time I was seated up on the stage, staring out at the football stadium full of thousands—literally, thousands—of unfamiliar faces, I was a good deal less cavalier. The TV camera bored a hole in my forehead. The red light was the devil's eye, winking at me. A few other people gave some speeches, which I didn't really listen to. I grew increasingly nervous, perspiring under my cheap polyester gown. Then my name was called, there was applause and a few catcalls, and I stepped up to the podium, clutching my three-by-five cards for dear life.

"Fellow graduates of the class of seventy-eight, Principal Osder, distinguished guests, family, friends . . ." I faltered, took a sip of water, and started again. "Today is the day—Today is the day—" I looked down at my notes. It was a soaring speech, full of trumpets and triumph and onward, sweet victory; and none of it was the truth. I had all sorts of mountaineering metaphors I'd intended to use at the start, about climbing the summit, scaling the peaks, and so on, but they all sounded like hackneyed drivel to me.

I looked out at the eager, upturned faces and picked out a

few that I recognized—faces I had come to know and even love over the past four years. Rhonda, grinning from ear to ear. My cheerleading squad. The Student Council. Miss Miller, who had let me skip class to write. Tiny Teena, sniffling in the back row. They all deserved better than this. Hell, I deserved better than this.

I coughed to cover up the uncomfortable silence, while a tremendous battle raged inside me: who was going to speak— me or the Black Beast? It was the same damned battle I'd fought since I was seven, and I could feel my hands begin to clench into the familiar, too-tight fists.

"Not now," I argued.

"Now," he insisted.

I closed my eyes, and the Black Beast opened them. He looked around at all the unsuspecting faces, and a savage pleasure swept through my body. So much undefiled innocence; so much experience to impart.

When I spoke, I barely recognized my voice. It was lower than my normal register, with an urgent vibrato underneath that could very well be mistaken for a growl. The slow, stately tempo felt strange, because usually when the Black Beast spoke, he talked so fast that people had difficulty understanding him. Now he—I—we—enunciated every word, every syllable.

"Today," I said, clutching the podium and staring fiercely at the little red light, "is nothing. It's—" I cast around feverishly in my mind for an appropriate metaphor, wishing to Christ I'd brought along some of those great Nietzsche quotes. But even if I couldn't remember the exact words, their emotional resonance still stayed with me. I seized on the lyrics of a popular song that had been nearing the top of the charts for the last few weeks: "—dust in the wind. That's all we are and all we'll ever be: dust in the wind."

I heard Principal Osder shifting nervously in his seat behind me, but the Black Beast kept on going. "No matter what accomplishments you think you have achieved, no matter where you go from here or what you ever do, you're dust, and the wind is always blowing. Even as you sit here today, it's blowing seconds of your life away. You might think you can stop it if you attend the right college, or get the right car, the right job, the right spouse, but you can't. You're just fooling yourself. The wind is always blowing."

"Terri—" Principal Osder whispered. I didn't turn around.

"Thousands of Chaffey graduates have come before us. Many more will follow. But mere numbers don't add up to spit. The only thing remotely special about today, the only possible beauty in these boring, worn-out ceremonies, lies in whatever personal message is received by each one of us, as unique individuals. The labels we've attached to ourselves can't do our living for us. We become dust in the wind the second we drift away from what we've made ours, from our own tiny but essential peculiarity."

Rivulets of sweat began to run down my forehead, stinging my eyes. I wiped them away and went on:

"So know this, if you know nothing else: happiness is for each person something totally different, and what matters most to each of you probably means nothing to anyone else. Look around you. I mean it: actually look to either side of you."

A confused murmur rose from the stadium. Faces turned nervously from side to side.

"Do they really care? Do they even know you, have you ever let yourself be seen? No. Understand that now, and you will save yourself a lifetime of grief. So let's ponder not the magic but the true insignificance of this moment: one more speck of dust, caught up in one last breeze."

And then, all at once, I ran out of words. The Black Beast had had his say, and he left me, as he always did, to deal with the consequences. "Thank you very much," I said, stepping back from the podium. I sat down next to Principal Osder and waited.

Silence, a vast echo chamber, a throb of empty air: nothing, not even a cough.

One Mississippi.

Two Mississippi.

Three Mississippi.

And then it started. A single, lonesome clap from somewhere out in the bleachers to the left of me. Followed by another, and another, and another until, in a rippling percussive wave, the single claps became applause. Polite at first, perhaps perfunctory, I thought: just a way to ease the tension. But no. The wave began to build until it swept the entire stadium. The air, which had vibrated with such uncertainty a few seconds earlier, resounded with whistles and cheers. The students got to their feet, followed by the audience, the teachers, even Principal Osder. I alone stayed seated, stunned. I'd expected boos and hisses and eventual censure; anything but a standing ovation.

Hadn't they heard a word I'd said? I felt like a criminal who, for the life of me, couldn't get caught.

Three months later, I was seated in row twenty-one on the red-eye to New York, waiting for my Vassar adventure to begin. My entire family had trooped out to the airport to see me off: my mother openly crying, my father's hands trembling a little as he slipped five hundred more dollars inside my purse "just in case." Even Zach looked a bit misty around the edges, although he pretended to be more interested in the airplanes than in me.

I was more than a little shaky myself, never having been farther than a hundred miles from home on my own before. It felt like that first day at Pomona College: "What will I do if I can't find the bathroom?" But although I was properly tearful for my family's benefit, inside I couldn't keep the excitement from bubbling over. I was finally leaving, getting the hell out, going far, far away from everything I was so certain was "wrong with me."

I boarded the plane, stowed my bag under the seat, and fastened my seat belt low and snug, just like the rules tell you to do. The stewardess walked by and smiled at me—a good omen, I thought. There would be plenty more smiles from here on in, if only I kept to my agenda. The graduation speech had taught me a lot: my instincts were all wrong, I realized. I could never, ever trust the Black Beast to do anything but get me into trouble.

Although my speech had been a wild success, it had frightened me to the core to hear words coming out of my mouth that I had never intended to say. I felt like I was walking on razor blades in thin-soled slippers. So from that day forward, I vowed to do everything differently. I even tried switching hands from right to left when I ate and wrote and blow-dried my hair, just to confound my natural instincts.

The engines whined, and we started to taxi. I'd flown many times before, but taking off always made me nervous. I reached into my purse and got out my mother's pearls—my pearls now, since to my utter surprise and delight she had given them to me as a graduation present. I stroked them, their cool, smooth opalescence soothing me, as it always had for as far back as I could remember.

As I fingered them in the motion so familiar to me from counting the rosary, I repeated my new vows silently to myself:

1. I will not try to be the best.
2. I will not compete.
3. I will not join in.
4. I will never again listen to the Black Beast.

The plane started to lift, and the g-force pressed me back against the seat. I looked out the window and watched the congestion of Los Angeles gradually disappear. As we banked over the ocean, all I could see, as far as forever, was the pure, serene blue of sea and sky. It was starting, the next chapter, the one I'd been waiting for all of my life. Everything would be different from here on in. Everything.

Inside me, the Black Beast smiled.

Epilogue

As anyone who has read *Manic* already knows, the Black Beast didn't stay behind in Ontario. He came with me to Vassar, then to UCLA Law School, and on into the wilds of my professional career as an entertainment litigator. But at Vassar, there was a qualitative difference to my life. While I broke almost every one of my vows the very first week I was there, I remained steadfastly faithful to one: I didn't join in. The years of me belonging to every organization, running every club, aspiring to every top clique, were over—never to return again.

In place of a normal social life, I discovered men. Whatever had been wrong with me at Chaffey High—out of place, undesirable, too much of or too little—was magically fixed the instant

I stepped foot on the East Coast (where, to my shock and delight, pale skin and flaming hair were considered a fascinating, not flawed, combination). I was asked out by the very first boy I met on campus, then another, and another. Tamped down for so long, the Black Beast's sexuality exploded into being, quickly followed by the exquisite imbalance of love. I was out of my head, off my rocker, delirious: all very familiar places to me, and not so uncommon at Vassar. A carefully honed eccentricity was the norm there, and as I suspected, I fit right in.

But much as I adored my college in theory, I noticed a troubling change in my moods. I didn't think it was possible, but the lows got even lower, the highs even higher. Part of the problem was New York City, a mere two hours away by train. Whatever mood I found myself in, the city trebled it. If I was blue, the city was indigo; I saw evidence of despair and desolation everywhere I looked. But if I was exuberant, the city was one big, glorious skyscraper. I gorged on art, I feasted, I feted, until even the Black Beast's enormous appetites were satisfied. It was impossible to live a nonchalant life surrounded by such a maelstrom.

Although I was reluctant to leave the East Coast, my parents divorced when I was at Vassar, and I felt it best to be closer to my mother, who was having a difficult time. I quickly learned that altruism is no guarantee of happiness. UCLA Law School was the biggest mistake I ever made. The Black Beast took one whiff of the place and plunged into a depression so severe and prolonged that I don't know how I survived it. For the very first time in my life, I embraced mediocrity, showing up at classes only to take the exams. My grades were abysmal, my attitude worse, and my life was a series of such extreme ups and downs, I felt perpetually seasick.

The nausea continued when I entered the law. The Black Beast loathed the professional straitjacket he was forced to wear, even though it was invisible and lined with gold and silver. I didn't care whether I lived or died, and so I lived with such recklessness that I shocked even myself.

You can't get better until you hit bottom, or so the wise men say. But my life was like a magician's cabinet, full of many false bottoms: several unsuccessful suicide attempts, followed by several ineffective hospitalizations. Yet I don't think I hit my personal nadir until my father died when I was thirty-seven. By then I had finally been diagnosed—first with major depression; then at last, properly, with bipolar disorder. But my father's long and brutal struggle with lung cancer made a mockery out of my own inveterate skirmish with moods. I remember looking at him in his hospital bed: withered, gray, emaciated; tubes sticking out of every orifice; his lovely silver hair all but gone from the chemo. "Top that," I said to the Black Beast, and he slunk away in shame.

But oh, did he come roaring back after my father died. As I chronicled in *Manic*, I sincerely tried to end my life on a trip to Santa Fe by taking of all of Daddy's leftover pain meds, plus my own stockpile of pills, plus as much tequila as my body could hold down. It was a valiant effort, to no avail. I lived to face yet another hospitalization, this time back at UCLA.

When you're depressed, the well-worn path can offer little hope. What I couldn't see from my dark vantage point was that

I was finally on the road to home: at UCLA, on the cusp of the new century, I picked up my pen and began to write my story.

I won't say that writing tamed the Black Beast. It soothed him, though, enough so that he agreed simply to occupy a corner of my mind. But I won't soft-pedal it: recovery is hard, and for the first few years, there were more lapses than progress. It took a synchronicity of resources to finally get me on track: the right diagnosis, the right medications, the right psychopharmacologist, the right therapist, two weekly writing groups, several mental health support groups, years of AA meetings, and long-term, vigilant sobriety. Gradually, I redirected my focus and skills toward causes much closer to my own heart: writing and mental health advocacy.

My manic episodes became fewer and more manageable, the consequences less dire. My depressions were not so malleable, though. They continued to haunt me, sometimes arriving strictly out of the blue, sometimes in response to stress. But each time was shorter and less severe, until a familiar four-day pattern emerged. While suicide still felt like a viable option, it wasn't a constant preoccupation.

By 2008, when *Manic* was published, I felt like I had found my rhythm at last. I was still bipolar, still clinically ill, still renting out space in my head to a beast. But I was doing what I loved best in life, and I felt more valuable as an author and advocate than I had ever felt as a lawyer. It mattered to me that I was alive.

In fact, with the unexpected success of my book, I felt so good at times that I even wondered, was I still bipolar? In my community work, I saw so many people who were much worse off than I was—deep in their disease in a way I no longer seemed to be. I knew that this often happens to manic-depressives: the brain forgets the ravages of the illness the way a woman forgets the pains of childbirth. You have to, to survive. But it's always a dangerous place to be, because you inevitably start to question the need for medication, therapy, and all the other rigorous stopgaps of sanity so carefully put into place to prevent another episode.

It troubled me so much that I asked my psychopharmacologist, "Tell me the truth. Am I really bipolar?" He smiled his subtle smile and said, "Yes, Terri, you're bipolar." I trusted his answer, and yet . . . It had been months since I'd felt a flicker from the Black Beast. All the emails regarding my book kept telling me what a brave, courageous, and evolved soul I was. The reviews made me sound like the poster child for bipolar recovery, all my struggles described in the past tense. I started, God help me, to believe my own publicity.

And then I went back home again.

It was Thanksgiving Day 2009. My mother and I had just had a lovely lunch at a nearby cafe. In her mideighties, she's still remarkably attractive, but frail; my escapades have worn her to a bit of a frazzle. With my father's death, the jealousy and animosity that once raged so fiercely between us has passed. We are both a little too old and too tired to muster up the energy to fight. And so we talk on the phone at least once a day and do our lovely lunches every now and then.

I'd gone home not just to visit her but to find out if there were any old photographs lying around that I might include in this book. We were never a picture-taking family, and so I doubted I'd find much. "Try that bureau," my mother said, pointing to an antique hutch in the living room. I hadn't opened it in years— one still does not open my mother's drawers without her express permission. Even then, one opens them at one's peril: avalanches of odds and ends come pouring out and never fit back in. She hoards the past as if it's gold, and she is God's appointed miser.

I tugged at a cupboard, and sure enough, a flood of miscellany spilled out all over the floor: bits of string and bags of rubber bands and bunches of dead flowers, a loving cup, old vinyl records, empty boxes, broken bagatelles. But mostly there were papers. Pages and pages and pages of papers—yellowing, faded, creased but preserved in dozens of files and envelopes marked "Important! Do Not Throw Away!!"

Curious, I opened a few. No photographs—nothing in my life is ever so simple as a static image. But I immediately recognized what I saw: my own words, from as far back as I could remember, in loopy crayon and later in pen, and later still in my father's neat typewriting. Hundreds of pages. I must have written every single day of my life. I must have written like a fiend. I must have howled like a beast.

There it was, sprawled all around me: poetry from my earliest days, all about death and dying and suicide, with titles like "Calamity" and "A Grave of Water" and "The End" and "Judgment Day." Poems so bleak and full of despair I couldn't read them without aching for the child who knew such things at ten; who felt such things at twelve. The manic poems were in there too, drunk on sounds and associations and dripping with wordplay. It was all there, all of it: evidence that even my rigid lawyer's brain had to admit as proof. I wasn't making a whit of it up. The Black Beast lived, and still lives, inside me.

My mother came in and asked me why I looked so upset. I handed her a poem: "The Gloom Everlasting." "Oh yes," she said, scanning it quickly and putting it down. "You always wrote beautiful poetry. Your father wanted so much to get it published." Then she went back into the kitchen to make me some chamomile tea.

As I continued to sort through the pages, my sorrow slowly disappeared, replaced by a mounting anxiety. It suddenly no longer felt safe to be there. I bundled up the poetry and told my mother I had to leave—I had an early appointment the next morning, or some other little white lie to hide the fact that the Black Beast was starting to scream inside me, the same old familiar seven words: "I have to get out of here."

I'm not sure how I made it home, an hour's drive away. I remember clutching the steering wheel so tightly that my fingers looked frostbitten. I didn't turn on the radio; I drove in silence, with the window down, even though it was a bitter night. I drove so fast that I almost outran the rhymes and rhythms that were chasing me. Almost.

When I reached my little bungalow in Benedict Canyon, a light shone through the window. It was all I wanted: to be safe inside, out of the cold and the dark. But my key wouldn't fit in the patio gate. (It was the wrong key, but I neither noticed nor cared.) Without a moment's thought, I kicked in the gate, splintering the rotten wood around the lock.

The minute that I stepped inside, it hit me: a shock wave of anger. I'd spent my entire childhood and adolescence worrying that there was something wrong with me. But what, in God's name, was wrong with *them*? All of them, starting with my beloved father and including all the adults who'd ever read and applauded my writing: my mother, the nuns, Father Tim, Professor Tremaine, all my teachers and mentors, that stadium full of people who had stood and cheered my bizarre graduation speech. All those relentless, fucking A-pluses, despite my prolonged absences from school and odd behavior. Had no one ever seen me?

I couldn't stop shivering. What would have happened if one of them, just one adult, had recognized and acted on the obvious: that however articulate, however poised, however accomplished, this child wasn't normal. My mother had come the closest, perhaps, but even she had never taken that last essential step and insisted I get help. Maybe that was why I was always the angriest with her—or maybe it was simply because she was so near to finding out and therefore presented the biggest threat.

The truth was, none of them had ever dared to look the Black Beast in the eye.

Still shaking, I peeled off my clothes, slipped into my thickest robe, and huddled in front of the heater. As the warmth slowly penetrated my body, the anger began to dissipate. It was succeeded by a deep regret, a big black lump of Christmas coal. In doing my research for this book, I've read over and over again about the importance of early intervention. Studies have repeatedly shown that it can really make a difference in early-onset bipolar disorder, significantly arresting the progress of the disease and reducing the number and severity of episodes.

I wanted—what? Revenge? Retribution? No. I wanted my childhood back.

Tears welled up, and I welcomed them. Over the course of these many years, I've learned an important lesson: melancholia has its value. Sadness is not depression. Tears can heal, or so I hoped as I wiped them off my cheeks, my chin. I was still able to think clearly, logically, as I picked the pieces out of the puzzle and tried to rearrange them into some semblance of order.

It wasn't my parents' fault—it was nobody's fault—that I was born with a chemical imbalance in my brain. It was a different time, a different world, when I was growing up. Commercials about bipolar disorder and depression didn't run nonstop on mainstream TV; there were no full-page ads in popular magazines; no best-selling memoirs. There was only shame—and silence.

And here was the trickiest piece of all: I, who knew the most and was closest to the secret, did my overachieving best to preserve and protect that silence. I didn't blame, I merely observed—I wasn't always held hostage. There were good days too, when I might have slipped into my father's lap and told him what was going on. He loved me, it's possible he might have understood. But I was too afraid back then. And now I'll never know.

It was a heartbreaking moment and yet, oddly enough, exhilarating too. I realized for perhaps the very first time that I was no longer that strangled child. I was no longer trapped in a cage of fear. *Manic* had liberated me, and now I had a voice that had reached across oceans. I grabbed my pen blindly through the tears and scribbled three words on a Post-it note: "Believe your child."

I was back to the beginning, to that very first impulse that had made me want—no, need—to write this book. To all the parents I wrote it for, to all the parents who are wondering, worrying, lost in the dark: please, don't let the silence triumph. Listen and learn and read and discover and most of all, believe your child. Name the Black Beast with impunity if he dares to show his face. If there's one thing I can claim to know, it's this: naming a beast is always the first step toward taming him.

Resources

A note regarding terminology: as recently as
the mid-1990s, bipolar disorder was thought to be extremely
rare in children, verging on nonexistent. The situation has
been changing rapidly—and along with it, the language used to
describe the illness. In order to properly research this subject,
it helps to know that the illness is currently known by several
different names: pediatric bipolar disorder, early-onset bipolar
disorder, juvenile bipolar disorder, childhood and adolescent
bipolar disorder.

In addition, a new diagnostic category—temper dysregulation
disorder with dysphoria (TDD)—has been proposed for the
2013 edition of the *Diagnostic and Statistical Manual of Mental*

Disorders, or *DSM-V,* the psychiatric bible relied upon by doctors and insurance companies. This alternative diagnosis, the source of considerable debate, is intended to apply to children who have explosive anger outbursts in response to commonplace events. In between the outbursts, the child experiences a persistent negative mood—a chronic irritability, as opposed to the elevated or euphoric symptoms often found in classic bipolar mania.

The following books proved invaluable to my own research and are very accessible to laypersons. They also provide extensive compilations of resources:

- *The Bipolar Child: The Definitive and Reassuring Guide to Childhood's Most Misunderstood Disorder* (3rd ed.) by Demitri Papolos, MD, and Janice Papolos (New York: Broadway Books), 2006.
- *Is Your Child Bipolar? The Definitive Resource on How to Identify, Treat, and Thrive with a Bipolar Child* by Mary Ann McDonald, APRN, BC, and Janet Wozniak, MD, with Judy Fort Brenneman (New York: Bantam Dell), 2008.
- *The Bipolar Teen: What You Can Do to Help Your Child and Your Family* by David J. Miklowitz, PhD, and Elizabeth L. George, PhD (New York: Guilford Press), 2008.
- *If Your Child Is Bipolar: The Parent-to-Parent Guide to Living with and Loving a Bipolar Child* by Cindy Singer and Sheryl Gurrentz (Glendale, Calif.: Perspective Publishing), 2003.

- *The Ups and Downs of Raising a Bipolar Child: A Survival Guide for Parents* by Judith Lederman and Candida Fink, MD (New York: Fireside), 2003.

I can also recommend the following organizations and their websites:

- The Bipolar Child (www.BipolarChild.com)— website maintained by the authors of *The Bipolar Child*; includes a newsletter and a model IEP (Individual Education Plan) for students struggling with bipolar disorder
- Child and Adolescent Bipolar Foundation (www .bpkids.org)—a parent-led organization for families with bipolar children
- International Bipolar Foundation (www .internationalbipolarfoundation.org)—publishes an excellent newsletter with cutting-edge research and information
- Juvenile Bipolar Research Foundation (www.jbrf .org)—a charitable organization focusing on research; website includes a Childhood Bipolar Questionnaire, information about clinical studies, and professional Listservs
- National Alliance on Mental Health (www.nami .org)—a particularly good resource for families and friends of loved ones with all types of mental

illness; conducts local support groups and training
sessions

- National Institute of Mental Health (www.nimh.
nih.gov)—the leading federal agency for research on
mental illness and mood disorders

Acknowledgments

First, I must thank the extraordinary number of
people who took the time and energy to write me about *Manic*,
or to attend one of my speaking engagements. You can't imagine
what it felt like to come out of the darkness into such light. My
heartfelt thanks to each and every one of you, and especially to
the parents of bipolar children, who inspired this book.

My love and gratitude go out to the following people (in
alphabetical order):

To Nancy Bacal, whose grace and wisdom have enriched
my writing for so many years. She is more than a teacher; she
is a docent to life. And to all the past and present members of
her Wednesday afternoon and Monday night groups, who have

listened so patiently to my pages and never once encouraged me to get a day job: Ann Bailey, Steve Brourman, Soo-Hyun Chung, Larry Downes, Stevie Ellison, James Fearnley, Juliet Green, Wes Hill, Kim Kowsky, Marilyn Levine, Maureen Miller, Linda Neal, Fawn Rogers, Adrienne Rosenthal, Paul Ryan, Janet Tamaro, Scott Warner. And a very special thank-you to my darlings Paul Mantee (my hero, who can't be summed up in words) and Arnold Pomerantz, for showing me the wonders of a well-lived life.

To Lisa Doctor, my canny and generous Tuesday night teacher, who has been so instrumental in helping me learn how to balance the dreams and realities of the writing life. And to our Tuesday night clan, who have endured my lousy first drafts without wincing and given me great friendship and support in return: the talented Linzi Glass, Cyndi Greening, Terry Hoffmann, Jeremy Iacone, Helena Kriel, Robert Rotstein, John Whelpley, Robert Wolff.

To Sarah Durand, my beloved and insightful editor, who always treats me with such respect and consideration, and who was brave enough to let my "Pre-Raphaelite angel" description of her remain in the Introduction.

To Le Pain Quotidien's Beverly Hills and Westwood branches, which allow me to scribble for hours on end over a single latte and a bowl of gazpacho and an order of five-grain bread. Thank you to all the waitstaff and managers, who have given me a home away from home.

To the brilliant and unsinkable Elyn Saks, with whom I'm writing my next book. She makes every Sunday morning at nine the brightest spot in my week.

To Dr. Harvey Sternbach, my steadfast psychopharmacologist, who has made an art form out of the science of medicating me, and who returns phone calls so quickly it makes my head spin.

To Dr. Geoffry White, my therapist for the past seventeen years, who has stood by me no matter what, no matter when. He is the essence of compassion, a genuine questioner who really wants to know the answers. Quite simply, I wouldn't be here if it weren't for him.

To Lydia Wills, my strong-souled agent at Paradigm, the poster child for chic. Without her belief in me, I'd still be staring at a blank page or, worse yet, practicing law.

To the impossibly debonair John Wolff, who knows everything and cares anyway. He has given me so much—a lifetime of memories, and the truest gift of all: forgiveness.

To Robert Young, master coach and pilot and counselor, whose love and loyalty made it possible for me to survive the cruelest years. We have shared a great adventure, and I owe him more than I can ever say.

And thank you to the following people, who have helped me so much along the way: Chris Blake, Sarah Cantin and Judith Curr at Atria, Dr. Jeff Davis, Suzy Davis, my copy editor Jonathan Evans, Sherrill Martin, Dr. Joan Osder, Gavin Polone, Sharyn Rosenblum, Dr. Rita Resnick, Elizabeth Suti.

Finally, thank you to my forever beautiful mother, for her strength and courage and unstinting love; and to my father, who, somewhere, is eating all this up with a spoon.